CW00672956

THE WAY WE WERE

A Bourne Society Book of Days

John D. Matthews

ISBN 0 900992 37 9

Cover Photograph

Marden Waggoner winning First Prize at the Shire Horse Show
— see 21st February 1933

THE WAY WE WERE: A BOURNE SOCIETY BOOK OF DAYS

Introduction

T HIS book aims to be the record of a year—not any particular year, but a composite year spanning the centuries of written records about the local area and its people. The items selected were all originally written down, with a precise date, in many different documents including State papers, local manorial court rolls, parish registers, private diaries, war diaries, newspapers etc. It is hoped that what emerges from this is a partial portrait of ordinary daily life over the years.

In compiling this collection it seems to me that, regardless of period or government, human nature varies little across recorded history: poaching, thieving, gambling, watering the beer and begetting children in and out of wedlock go on forever, side by side with acts of charity, attempts at improving the lot of oneself and others, and making the best of difficult circumstances. As in everyone's daily life, it appears that there are some days in the year where things happen, and are recorded, in great number, whilst on others almost nothing occurs.

In 1752 this country changed from the Julian to the Gregorian calendar, the latter still being in use. Under the former the civil and legal New Year's Day was Lady Day (25th March), which means that dates between 1st January and 24th March which we would now place in one year were, at the time, referred to as being in what we would consider to be the previous year.

Detailed sources have not been given for every item as to do so would have taken almost as much space as the daily entries themselves, but where it seems necessary in order to make sense of an item, the source is indicated in brackets; where the general source is implicit in what is being said, then it is not quoted against the entry. However, a general list of sources is given at the end.

Hopefully, some amongst you may like to follow up some of the items and enlarge upon them, perhaps in future Bourne Society publications.

Finally, I would like to thank all those who assisted me in collecting the information for this "Book of Days."

Thanks are also due to the following for permission to reproduce their photographs: Croydon Advertiser Group Limited, Croydon Libraries, Museum & Arts, Croydon Natural History and Scientific Society, East Surrey Museum, E.P. Humphreys, The Trustees of the Imperial War Museum, London, Roger Packham and Dorothy Tutt; and to Liz Malarkey for photography.

Original spellings and idiosyncrasies of style have been retained.

John D Matthews

JANUARY

1st 1643 Baptism in Sanderstead of "Grace Taylor daughter of Joane Taylor (a vagrant) and (as she saith) of John Taylor her husband de Maydestone in the County of Kent."

1717 The parish of Warlingham collected 7s 6d for a Brief for "Churches in great Poland and Polish Prussia." (A Brief was a letter patent issued by the Sovereign as Head of the Church licensing a collection in the churches throughout England for a specified object of charity.)

1884 The last meeting of the Chipstead Manor Court.

1894 The diary of Solomon Windross of Beech Farm in Chelsham (hereinafter referred to as the "Beech Farm Diaries") recorded that "Tom Sales came to kill a pig which weighed 42 stone. Palmer had 125 lbs of pork at 3/7 per stone (£2 16 0½) also 31 lbs of Pigs Head 3d per lb (7/9)."

1912 Arthur Beadell, naturalist of the Chelsham/Warlingham area, recorded in his Nature Notes that "Gorse in flower at Worms Heath. Hazel catkins fully expanded at Searchwood Road. Pair of goldcrests seen at Broadlands."

2nd 1934 Godstone Sunday School children, having had their Prize Giving and Tea on New Year's Day, gave a repeat performance of the pantomime "Rumpelstiltskin", at 6 p.m. in the Whyte Hart Barn, "to raise a little money for Sunday School equipment and the rent of the Barn on Sunday mornings." (Godstone Parish Magazine)

3rd 1342 Andrew Peverel of Chelsham Court was appointed Sheriff of Surrey and Sussex.

1627 Henry Smith, alderman of the City of London, died aged 79. He was one of the greatest philanthropists of Stuart times, from whose generosity nearly every parish in Surrey, and others elsewhere, benefited—and still benefit. He is buried in Wandsworth parish church.

4th 1251 A grant was issued at Westminster to Roger St John giving him "free warren in his lands in his manor of Welkested Surrey (i.e. Godstone) and of a weekly market there on Friday and a yearly fair on the vigil, the feast and the morrow of St Nicholas." (Calendar of Charter Rolls)

5th 1360 At Reading King Edward III appointed "John and Philip Prophete to be masters and keepers of the quarries of Merstham and Chaldon by Reigate with power to select and dig and shape the stones in the quarries for the king's works in the castle of Windsor, and to arrest such as are contrariant or rebellious." (Calendar of Patent Rolls)

6th 1900 "The Chelsham and Farley school children enjoyed their Christmas tea and tree at the Ledgers. It takes no Attendance Officer to get a full muster for that, and the teachers must have wished that they could reckon as certainly on seeing the children at school as they can on a treat. After tea in the coach-house a move was made to the barn of many uses, where the tree in truly gorgeous splendour was ablaze with candles. After the numerous company had been made happy and grateful with presents they were amused before separating by a revival of the play mentioned above" ("Ici on parle francais".) (Warlingham and Chelsham Parish Magazine)

7th 1645 Phinehas Darknolls, rector of Titsey, wrote in the parish register that "George Leshley, soldier under Captain Hawes of Col. Rich's Regimt. came to free quarter at mine house, horse and man. Mr Leshley went away Jan 22 pd 8s."

1871 The *Croydon Advertiser* reported that "The unusually severe weather of the past three weeks has caused many labourers and mechanics to be out of work. Some of the well-to-do inhabitants of Catherham have generously contributed towards the opening of two soup kitchens, one at Upper Catherham and the other in the Valley, where soup is supplied to necessitous persons every Tuesday and Friday at 1d per quart. The soup is certainly excellent, and great credit is due to the persons who superintend the making of it. Upwards of 60 gallons is made each day."

1936 The Lantern Lecture delivered to the Caterham Literary Society was "Treasure Hunting in the Cocos Islands" by Commander Worsley. He had in the past commanded 21 vessels including Sir Ernest Shackleton's Antarctic ships *Endurance* and *Quest* and 5 warships.

8th 1643 The burial took place in Titsey of "Reginald Short of Smeede in Kent, a Parliament soldier of Captain Scott's trayne of horse, dying at the Lady Gresham's, where he was quartered."

1894 Kenley National School reopened after the Christmas holiday. The Log Book says that there was "A very poor attendance - weather intensely cold. Schoolroom most uncomfortable. At 8.30 the Thermometers stood respectively at 32 degrees & 31 degrees and in the Infants Room at 30 degrees. At 9.45 the Thermometers in the Main Room stood at 42 & 40. In Infants Room with gas on at 40 degrees."

9th 1275 The Abbot of Hyde in Winchester brought a case before King Edward I at Marlborough "against Henry, Prior of Bermondsey, and 14 others" accusing them of "trespass in a case concerning making divisions between the lands of the Prior in Warlingham and the Abbot's lands in Sanderstead." (Calendar of Close Rolls)

1989 The start of the replanting of trees in the Promenade de Verdun, Woodcote, where the originals had been badly damaged in the storm of October 1987.

10th 1828 The Caterham churchwardens "paid Nathaniel Brooke for clearing the paths in the Church Yard:- 4s.0d."

1904 A "Toy Service" at St Mary's Church Caterham, was postponed for a week "on account of the wet weather." (See 17th January 1904)

11th 1941 The A.R.P. Report Post in Bletchingley recorded the dropping of a "Molotov Breadbasket" on Coldharbour and South Park at 20.00 hours. No damage was done and there were no casualties.

12th 1596 Before a grand jury at Croydon sessions Alice Marten (or Tosby), a spinster of Bletchingley, was indicted for witchcraft. It was presented that she had bewitched to death, at Bletchingley, an ox (worth £3), a ram (6s 8d), a sheep (6s) and a lamb (10d) belonging to Edward Tyrry on 30th April 1593. She was found not guilty.

1871 A Servants' Ball took place at the Salmons in Whyteleafe, whose owner, G.W.P. Woodroffe Esq, allowed "his servants the privilege of inviting any of the tradesmen or friends they may be acquainted with. There was rather a large company present numbering upwards of 80. The hall was tastefully embellished with suitable devices and everything done to secure the comfort of the guests. Dancing commenced at nine in the evening and was kept up with unflagging spirit until six the following morning led by an efficient Quadrille Band from London. Mr and Mrs Woodroffe and visitors graced the festivities with their presence and appeared to take a lively interest in the proceedings." *(Croydon Advertiser)*

1886 "John Mears who is a very naughty troublesome boy was kept in....his mother came to the Master's house in the evening & was abusive! -'You nasty old devil'." (Kenley National School Log Book)

13th 1269 Chertsey abbey archives contain a final agreement of this date under which Joel de la Garston and Philippa his wife conveyed a messuage and a carucate of land called Garston (in Watendon) to Roger and Matilda de Harve. The payment for this was 80 marks of silver (£53 6s 8d) plus the customary rent for these premises of one halfpenny, payable every Easter at Coulsdon church.

1766 A very precise entry in the Coulsdon parish registers says that Toby, the son of John Caulfield (curate of Coulsdon) and his wife Euphemia, was born "exactly at half an hour past three in the morning."

1823 "My second son's 21st birthday, Gilbert. Dined forty five persons in the large greenhouse. With the people who came in afterwards we were one hundred and eight. Danced to 5 a.m."(Diary of Mrs William Jolliffe of Merstham.)

14th 1936 The Caterham Literary Society Lantern Lecture was *The Blue Danube: Black Forest to Black Sea on a Bicycle!!* by Bernard Newman Esq. The talk described "A lone journey across seven countries; strange pictures of unknown Europe. Adventures with Gypsies, wolves, vampires and - Rumanian Police!"

15th 1579 William Wodden was fined 6d at the manor court for illegally killing the rabbits belonging to William Goodwine, using traps, in Warlingham.

1895 "The 'quarterly' Tea and Entertainment in connection with the Band of Hope took place at the Mission Room on Tuesday, January 15th. Though it usually is only held once a year, it is called quarterly because it is so in intention at least." (Warlingham and Chelsham Parish Magazine)

16th 1941 "19.50 - 20.00: Gas mask practice for Report Centre staff. 20.55: C Division H/Q ask if Wardens should sound whistles in event of I.B. attack" (i.e. Incendiary Bomb). "Reply in Negative. 21.00: Clock corrected. B.B.C news - Wardens to use whistles, in London Civil Defence Region, to give warnings of I.Bs. Compulsory evacuation, in Greater London area, of children under 14 suffering from enemy attack. Local authorities empowered to have children medically examined." (Red to White Log Book of the Caterham and Warlingham Urban District Report and Control Centre, situated below the Soper Hall in Caterham) *(Plate I)*

17th 1804 Burial in Warlingham of "Richard White (Labourer, by excessive Drinking) aged 44."

1904 The "Toy Service" postponed a week earlier took place at St Mary's Church in Caterham. "The Service was attended by a very large number of children, who came laden with gifts. In all between four and five hundred toys were presented which were sent off next day to gladden the hearts of many little children in various hospitals and homes." (St Mary's Church Magazine)

1934 The Godstone Choir and Bellringers Outing was to see *The Mikado* at Streatham Theatre. About 50 people from Godstone and South Godstone went, the cost being around £12. "We shall probably revert next summer to the char-a-banc trip."

1936 Mr J. Chuter Ede, M.P.,D.L.,J.P., C.A.,Chairman of the Surrey County Council, formally opened The Caterham Hill Central School at 7 p.m.

18th 1656 A brief (or collection) was made in Bletchingley parish for Mr Honeywood and Henry Chesster, two English gentlemen who had been prisoners of "the Turks."

1892 The Misses Catherine and Winifred Pye opened their Eothen School in Caterham, with eight pupils.

19th 1862 "John Dalton vicar of Warlingham died, aged 67, and whatever his failings may have been, he certainly was not an absentee like many of his predecessors. On looking over the church accounts of the previous ten years, one cannot help noting the very frequent entry of charges for sacramental wine, in fact the annual average was nearly double the present (1900) expense, while the receipts from church rates was about £13." (Warlingham and Chelsham Parish Magazine)

1871 Police Constable Brooksbank, on accidentally hearing that John Stewart alias John Lambert had been offering fowls for sale to tradesmen, and in view of the recent spate of fowl robberies, sought him out in a neighbouring hostelry. He found him "smoking his pipe and doubtless enjoying some of the proceeds of his booty. His answers to the officer's questions were so unsatisfactory that he was at once taken into custody. Upon being searched, six fowls were found upon him. On his way to the magistrate's office he confessed that he had stolen the fowls." Tandridge bench of magistrates sentenced him to two months imprisonment, with hard labour, in Maidstone Gaol. *(Croydon Advertiser)*

20th 1892 "Mr A.F. Barron, FRHS, from the Royal Hort. Socy's Gardens, Chiswick, and his wife visited the School this afternoon to make a few enquiries about a boy named Albert Best, who, as an orphan, receives an allowance per week from the Gardener's Orphanage Fund towards his keep. The boy's conduct has not been of the best, but now the home circumstances are altered, I trust there will be a corresponding improvement in his conduct. Mr Barron, for the Committee, asked me to give an eye to the boy, which I readily consented to do, and also to receive the quarterly payments and to report to the Committee from time to time anything in connection with the boy deserving their attention." (Kenley National School Log Book)

21st 1939 The programme showing at the Capitol Cinema in Caterham was *The Barretts of Wimpole Street* starring Norma Shearer, Charles Laughton and Frederic March plus Warner Oland in *Charlie Chan in Shanghai.*

22nd 1895 The start of a very cold and frosty period of weather. (See 8th February 1895)

1903 "Paid 15s for a Trap license. Paid Mr Tilley for 30 gallons of cider and 2 casks at 15/-: £2 5s 0d." (Account Book of John Sherwill of Layfield Farm, Chipstead)

23rd 1924 An auction took place in the Y.M.C.A. Hut, which stood in the grounds of the East Surrey Water Works in Purley, of the Hut itself, the Contents and additional outbuildings. The Contents included "2 Stoves, Striking Clock, the Apparatus of 2 W.C.s, 2 Lavatory Basins, 18 Collapsible

Tables, 150 Chairs, 10 Folding Card Tables, a Caterer's Iron Boiler, about 250 Yards of Linoleum and other effects." *(Plate II)*

24th 1596 A Southwark labourer, William Mosse, was indicted for burgling the house of John Pocknell at Tandridge and stealing 54 yards of woollen cloth worth £5. Roger Hunt, a tailor from Oxted, was charged as an accessory. Both were found guilty but were allowed clergy.

1920 *The Croydon Advertiser* reported that "A storm of disapproval has been aroused by the suggestion that the Y.M.C.A. hut near Purley Terminus is no longer required for the entertainment of soldiers and that it might be utilised for housing during the present shortage. Soldiers and civilians flock to the hut for the weekend concerts."

25th 1554 Sir Thomas Cawarden, Master of the Revels at Court and Keeper of the Tents, Hales and Toyles to Henry VIII, was arrested at his house in Bletchingley by Lord William Howard and James and John Skinner. He was taken before the privy council in Star Chamber because it was thought that he was likely to join Thomas Wyatt's rebellion against Mary Tudor and her planned marriage to Philip of Spain.

1820 The baptism took place in Sanderstead of "William Purley, found in Purley in this parish, aged about six months." The Rector, The Revd John Courtney, adopted him, brought him up and sent him to college. He became a clergyman, taking the name of Courtney, and went to the Isle of Wight to work.

1929 The Purley Sub-Division of the Metropolitan Special Constabulary Reserve held its 1st Annual Dinner and Smoking Concert at the *Railway Hotel* in Purley. The entertainment included music, singing and recitation, and Mr Humphrey Griffiths, a member of the Magic Circle, performed Conjuring and Sleight-of-Hand. *(Plate III)*

26th 1554 Sir Thomas Cawarden was discharged and given two letters by the privy council: one told the sheriff, Thomas Saunders, to vacate Cawarden's house, which he had occupied since the day before, and the other ordered Cawarden to make military preparations to oppose Wyatt's rebellion (having been arrested on 25th suspected of being a probable rebel!) Cawarden was already licensed to keep 40 retainers, and he had at Bletchingley enough arms and equipment to outfit as many as 110 Horse and 300 Foot. He also had 16 pieces of ordnance.

27th 1554 Lord William Howard (the lord admiral of England) sent word to Sir Thomas Cawarden to meet him a mile distant from his house in Bletchingley, obviously not wishing to confront him in the presence of his well-armed retinue. Curiously, Cawarden went to the meeting—and was arrested again, Howard declaring that he had "authority to seize the arsenal at Blechingley for the Queen's use."

1893   "Went to Godstone Board of Guardians with Mr Jarvis. Annie drove to meet him and Polly fell down and threw her out but hurt neither of them, only broke the cart a little" (Beech Farm Diaries)

1945   *The Croydon Times and Surrey County Mail* carried the following advertisement for Purley Ice Rink:
"Sessions daily 2.30 to 5 p.m. and 7 p.m. to 9.45 p.m.
Skaters 2/6 - including hire of boots and skates 3/-
Skaters H.M. Forces 1/9 - including hire of boots and skates 2/6
Skaters Children 1/9 - including hire of boots and skates 2/3
Spectators 1/- (including tax)".

28th 1596   Gabriel Couchman, a Croydon yeoman, was accused of having on this day, with others, committed highway robbery at Smithambottom. He was indicted for assaulting John Boulden and Edward Chittye and stealing a silver spoon worth 6 shillings, a girdle and a dagger (6s), a cloak-bag (6s), a cloak (£2), a shirt (10s), 2 shirtbands (10s) and 17s.1d in cash. He was found not guilty.

29th 1554   Lord Howard sent Sir Thomas and William Saunders and their men to seize Cawarden's armoury (see above, 26th January)—they took away 18 wagonloads of weapons and other gear. (After his subsequent release Cawarden, despite his strenuous efforts, only succeeded in getting 4 cartloads returned to him.)

1703   Bletchingley churchwardens collected £4 14s for the relief of "the Poor distressed Protestants" driven out of the Principality of Orange by the French King.

1910   At about 4.30 p.m. a Brighton to London express train was partially derailed at the points at Stoats Nest Station. Six passengers and a man standing beside the track were killed. Invaluable help was given by the Purley, Coulsdon and District Boy Scout Troop ("Princess Christian's Own"), who were playing football in a nearby field. The Chief Scout awarded the movement's Medal of Merit to the entire Troop.

30th 1931   Advance notice was given in *The Times* that the Imperial Ice Rink in Brighton Road, Purley, would be opened on 5th February by Sir Arthur Duckham. Miss Kathleen Shaw, the lady champion figure skater of Great Britain, and Mr J.F. Page, the champion, with other well-known skaters, would give exhibitions during the opening evening.

31st 1781   Coulsdon parish registers contain a copy of a letter written on this day by the Revd Mr Manning of Godalming to the Revd Mr Edmund Ferrers answering the latter's query, made on behalf of the Coulsdon rector, Mr Goodricke, about the location of, and historical records relating to, the church in the Watendon manor in Coulsdon which was mentioned in Domesday Book. (The site of the Watendon church was located and excavated by the Bourne Society in 1966.)

1942 "Angmering 0900 - Lieut G. Payette proceeded on secret and urgent duty to Caterham where it was later announced he married a young English Lady." (War Diary Royal 22e Regiment, Canadian Active Service Forces)

FEBRUARY

1st 1901 "School closed all day; all business being suspended tomorrow, owing to the funeral procession through London of our late Queen, Victoria, many of the children will be wanted at home." (Kenley National School Log Book)

2nd 1682 Anne Bassett was buried in Farleigh. The register includes a "Memorandum that the Affidavit concerning her being buried in Woollen was not brought to me before the 12th day of this month, concerning which I gave notice to William Allingham, churchwarden of this Parish the 15th day of Febr." (The Woollen Act of 1678 required that corpses be buried only in shifts, shrouds etc. made of wool, and an affidavit was made at each burial to confirm that this had been observed. The aim was to lessen the importation of linen from "beyond the seas" and the encouragement of the English wool trade.)

1916 The Bourne began to flow through Purley and did not cease until 24th July. The greatest flow was on 12th April when about eight million gallons of water were registered at the water works.

3rd 1906 "Purrs from Purley, by Persian" wrote in the *Croydon Advertiser* that "The Brighton Motor Way Bill is marked 'dead' for the coming Session, at which there is rejoicing on Peaks Hill."

1915 Alderman G.A. Hardy J.P., L.C.C., gave a lantern slide lecture in the not quite completed Warlingham Church Hall. It was entitled *In the Trail of the Kaiser's Huns*—front seats were one shilling, others 6d and 3d. The proceeds went towards providing skylight blinds "rendered necessary by the danger from the air."

4th 1871 *The Croydon Advertiser* reported on Caterham's problems: "Numerous have been the depredations here of late. A few nights since, a pig was stolen from a sty belonging to J. Lawrence Esq of Mattville. Not the slightest clue has yet been obtained as would lead to the apprehension of the guilty party."

5th 1262 At Westminster Henry III granted a "Licence to Roger St John to fortify his house of Lageham in Walkested with a dyke, stockades and a paling, and for his heirs to keep it so, so long as they are faithful to the king." (Calendar of Patent Rolls)

1883 The Corporation of London completed the purchase of the four "Coulsdon Commons"—Farthing Down, Coulsdon Common, Kenley Common and Riddlesdown—for £7,000 from Edmund Byron, the last resident lord of the manor of Coulsdon.

1918 *The Times* reported that the house of W.J. MacCaw M.P. at Rooksnest Park, Godstone, had been raided by police after a tip-off from a dismissed maidservant that he was hoarding food, against the wartime regulations. He was—and was subsequently fined £400.

6th 1912 "Gnats on wing at 10 a.m. Thaw set in today - after most severe frost - which seemed to wake all nature up. Skylarks and hedgesparrows singing. Large seagull passed over Warlingham flying a very low zigzag course due south." (Arthur Beadell's Nature Notes)

1925 "Mr Gerald Marcuse of Caterham Hill, the amateur wireless operator, was the first man to get in touch with the Hamilton Rice Expedition in the Amazon, and delivered a message from the expedition to the Royal Geographical Society on Friday. (*The Times* on Monday 9th)

7th 1613 "I sent a warrant for Richard Botley" *[probably of Oxted]* "for suspicion aboute sheepe and lambs and for his dogg for kylling lambs and in serch the Constable found a peece" *[probably a fleece]* "I took it and sent him for his dogg to be hanged, and for him to finde suerty for the Sessions." ("Notebook of a Surrey Justice" by Bostock Fuller, hereinafter referred to as Bostock Fuller J.P.)

1881 An immature female Rough-Legged Buzzard "was trapped by a keeper named Martin in a small shaw near Chelsham Court. This bird was seen repeatedly in the neighbourhood and was at last caught in a gin baited with a rabbit which it had killed & left half-eaten, and to which it returned."

1925 "A spark from a passing train set fire on Saturday to a portion of the Purley Downs Golf Course near Croydon." (*The Times* on Monday 9th)

8th 1895 The frost had continued without a break since January 22nd, according to the Chelsham and Warlingham Parish Magazine: "The lowest temperature recorded at the Vicarage was in the early morning of February 8th when it was 3 degrees *[Fahrenheit]* below zero (= 35 degrees of frost). The thermometer in the air, being unaccustomed to such cold weather, unfortunately got jammed at the critical moment, but it would seem that the air temperature at Warlingham was less cold than at Purley and other places."

1895 The same magazine also reported a "tea and entertainment for the parish" on the same day: "The whole thing went off splendidly, children and parents alike thoroughly enjoying themselves. The entertainment, which began at 6.30, was given entirely by the children and the younger teachers."

9th 1611 Richard Kempsall of Bletchingley accused "Thomas Hayward and others for hunting and killing his conyes in his enclosed ground on Sundaye the xxvjth of the month of January last contrarye to the lawe" (Bostock Fuller J.P.)

1613 Elizabeth Lye was sent "to the gaole by the Constable of Caterham for Wylfull burning certaine bedding and other goods of Mr Best in his house" in Caterham. (Bostock Fuller J.P.)

10th 1430 William Uvedale the younger of Titsey was appointed Sheriff of Surrey and Sussex.

1905 "Mr Bustow Waleen of Croydon came down specially to give a lecture on Temperance to the children of St Mary's Band of Hope. There was a splendid attendance, as there had been all season." (Caterham - St Mary's Church Magazine)

1920 At 2.30 p.m., in Old Broad Street, London, the sale took place of the property formerly known as Fosterdown Fort in Caterham. Comprising 12 acres of well wooded land, two cottages, a brick store house and a sunken yard and stores containing 7 large store rooms, a small store passage and lobbies, it was being sold by the War Office as an eligible site for a residence, a sanatorium or a public institution.

11th 1673 In Chipstead the burial took place of "Francis Hatcher, aged an hundred years."

1905 "The *Caterham Weekly Press* called attention to the very thin attendance at the Caterham Club this winter. Here is a splendid Club-house, with two billiard rooms, a games room, a reading room, bath room and a lawn at the back. Any town might be proud of it, yet men here seem to have no use for it." (St Mary's Church Magazine)

12th 1687 Farleigh parish registers record the Christening of "Elizabeth Daughter of Elizabeth Constable, a base borne Child, the reputed father being John Bullin, who ran away."

1916 No.1 Vol.1 of *The Wipers Times or Salient News*, (the divisional trench journal of the 12th Battalion Sherwood Foresters, produced by Capt. F.J. Roberts and printed in a rat-infested cellar in the front line Ypres Salient) included a poem called "Night Hawks", one verse of which is:

> "Here Foresters make nightly play,
> And in the mud hold revel high
> Recalling fancy stunts performed
> At Shoreham, and at Bletchingly."

13th 1949 Hubert E. Pounds, ornithologist, recorded that "unusually large numbers of Fieldfares together with flocks of Redwings were present in the Farleigh-Addington district during the afternoon. I watched one huge straggling band composed of at least 400 birds as it moved sedately over in a north easterly direction."

14th 1883 The manager of the London & County Banking Company Limited in Reigate wrote a letter today to Mr R Martin, marked 'private', for his "opinion as to the probability of a person succeeding in Caterham Valley in opening a Middle Class Boarding & Day School. The terms are about £40 per annum Boarders & from £3.3.0 to £4.4.0 per term Day Boys..... have you any House at a moderate price that would do.....it is for a brother of mine. We came over about a year ago & liked the place very much."

1903 St Mary's Church in Caterham was fitted with new gas pendants and incandescent system.

15th 1886 "A new School Attendance Officer called today & took a list of irregular attenders. He seems pretty sharp, so perhaps something will be done to improve matters. The Attendance Officer's visit does not seem to have pleased some of the parents as some of them are inclined to be abusive and several messages were sent through their children to the teachers this afternoon." (Kenley National School Log Book)

16th 1941 "Woldingham - a free Concert was put on for the troops at the Capitol Theatre at Caterham, by a Troop from the Windmill Theatre, London." (War Diary West Nova Scotia Regiment)

1974 The Regal Cinema in Purley closed, its last film being *Don't Look Now.*

17th 1894 The Chelsham and Warlingham Parish Magazine's weather report for the month recorded only light rainfall, and "only on one day, the 17th, was there a fall of any magnitude. Last year, February was a much wetter month with rain falling on twenty-four days out of twenty-eight."

18th 1912 "Primroses & chickweed in flower. Hive bees abroad." (Arthur Beadell's Nature Notes)

1941 At 18.30—H.R.H. the Duke of Gloucester and numerous Staff Officers "attended a concert at Warlingham Hospital. It was a French Canadian Folklore Concert given by the soldiers of our unit with the help of English Girls all dressed in gay, colored French Canadian Costumes." (War Diary Royal 22e Regiment)

19th 1784 "George Cooper buried. This child's throat was cut with a razor by old Dame Kerrill in a fit of lunacy Feb 14, 1784." (Coulsdon parish register)

1903 "Mr Thimbleby insured 3 mares against foaling: £4 11s 3d." (Account Book of John Sherwill of Layfield Farm, Chipstead) *(Plate IV)*

20th 1915 The volunteer 'Croydon Riflemen', consisting of members of local Miniature Rifle Clubs who, for whatever reason, were not eligible to join the regular forces, were affiliated to the Central Association of Volunteer Training Corps. (See also 8th March 1915 and 16th December 1917)

1935 A Fancy Dress Carnival was held at the Imperial Ice Rink, Purley. The writer of Vol. 1 No. 7 of *The Imperial Magazine* "stood in the foyer and watched so many wonderful creations steadily coming in. For originality and variety this Carnival would certainly take some beating....The sorting of the votes for the prizes was a proper algebraic equation."

21st 1827 "After dinner, Sir William and Mr William went out for a long time to see if anyone was about the Great House, as someone had broken into it the night before, but did not carry off anything. Sir Edward Banks and Mr William bought two steamships, the *George IV* and the *Duke of York*." (Diary of Mrs William Jolliffe of Merstham)

1933 The three years old Shire stallion, Marden Waggoner, bred by Sir Bernard Greenwell Bart at Marden Park in Woldingham, won First Prize on the first day of the Shire Horse Show at the Royal Agricultural Hall, Islington. *(Cover plate)*

22nd 1962 Mr Wm Martingell, former Head Gardener to Arthur Hood, wrote to Coulsdon and Purley's Chief Librarian in response to a query about his former employer, who had been Chairman of the Royal Dental Hospital. He said that Mr Hood was a "descendant of the great Admiral Hood. Parts of his garden were called upper deck, quarter deck etc." He had been a Coulsdon churchwarden, living at Woodcroft in Hawkhirst Road before moving, in 1916, to Woodcroft in Hayes Lane, Kenley.

1979 Tandridge Council passed the Estimates to convert No. 1 Stafford Road, Caterham, into the East Surrey Museum. Plans had been prepared, tenders sought and planning permission granted by Surrey County Council. (See 10th May 1980 and 23rd Nov 1978)

23rd 1905 The 37th, and last, A.G.M. of the Caterham Gas Company was held at the Guildhall Tavern. A dividend of 9% was recommended for payment. An Extraordinary General Meeting followed "at which shareholders were told that a Bid was at that time being promoted in Parliament to provide for the transfer of the Caterham & District Gas Company to the Croydon Gas Company."

24th 1323 A letter in with the Coulsdon parish register says that "Peter de Purley & Iulian his Wife had Licence for their Chapel in their mansion at Holegh in Coulsdon."

1912 "Two kind friends have made it possible for the Vicar and Mrs Fergus Wood to enjoy the fulfilment of a long standing desire to visit Rome.

They leave on January 29th and possibly return on February 24th." (St John's Church Magazine—Caterham Valley)

25th 1939 *The Daily Telegraph* reported that the Caterham A.R.P. Committee had submitted plans to the Home Office to "construct an evacuation camp to house some thousands of Londoners in time of war at Godstone, Surrey, with underground shelters in the neighbouring Godstone Caves." The stone quarries, locally called caves, were described as being about eight miles in length, with entrances naturally camouflaged by trees, containing springs of drinking-quality water and deep enough to "provide complete protection against the heaviest bombs known."

1989 A Lebanon Cedar was planted at Watendon to replace the 300 years old cedar that came down in the October 1987 storm.

26th 1896 There was a severe frost from 22nd to 27th February in Warlingham, the lowest temperature being this morning, when it was 16 degrees Fahrenheit.

1934 The Regal Cinema opened, beating the Astoria in the race to be Purley's first picture palace by a few weeks. It seated 1,578 and the first film shown was *Building a Building* (a Mickey Mouse cartoon), followed by the features *I Live with You* and *Her First Mate*.

27th 1803 In Merstham Elizabeth Sageman was buried. She had died on Feb 24th, aged 101. Her disorder was described as "old age".

1965 The Bourne Society's ninth Annual General Meeting, held at St John's Church Hall in Caterham, heard two lectures. The first was on 'The Work of the Ordnance Survey', and the second was entitled 'How to Save the Relics of Our Recent Past.' The annual subscription, which could be paid at the meeting, was 10/-.

28th 1894 The Chelsham and Warlingham Parish Magazine said that today "an aurora borealis is reported to have been seen between 7 and 9 o'clock in the evening."

1895 The Parish Magazine reported that in Warlingham "The Soup Kitchen was this year open on ten occasions from January 30th to February 28th and we must thank Mrs Rowe once again for the trouble she took and the excellent soup she turned out. The soup was sold at 1d per quart."

1900 Relief of Ladysmith, after a lengthy siege. Private James Watts of Farningham Road, Caterham, was subsequently awarded a medal for his part in the defence. (He served in South Africa, Somaliland and, later, on the Western Front.)

29th 1604 Death of John Whitgift (who was nicknamed by Queen Elizabeth I "her little black husband"!) As well as being Archbishop of Canterbury he was also the lord of the manor of Croham, which included much of Sanderstead. (See 31st October 1601)

1892 "Fine morning some snow storms. Two men ploughing 1 getting flints. Palmer & Shanks dressing wheat. Pollie the pony not well." (Beech Farm Diaries) *(Plate V)*

MARCH

1st 1661 At the Surrey Quarter Sessions three Tandridge yeomen, John Rye, John Bennett and Richard Godsmarke, were charged with having, on this day, "made riot, battery, assault and affray there on George Gruner."

1765 Sir Kenrick Clayton, Bart, of Marden Park, leased to John Steel, a yeoman of Chailey in Sussex, the premises known as Lodge House or North Park House in Bletchingley together with arable land, meadows and woodland in Bletchingley, Godstone and Caterham. The lease was for 21 years, at an annual rent of £135 to be paid on Ladyday and Michaelmas, plus "2 couple of fat capons and 2 fat geese" to be delivered to Marden at Christmas. Clayton retained the right to have all the timber and the freedom to hunt, hawk and fish on the leased property.

2nd 1871 Frederick Snelling, while collecting orders in Warlingham for Mr Peters, butcher, of Caterham Valley, had an arm and a leg badly hurt when his horse suddenly became unmanageable and reared and fell on him. He was quickly taken to his home in Upper Caterham, where Dr Hooper found that he luckily had no bones broken. *(Croydon Advertiser)*

1892 "Very stormy snowy day. Men carting wood from 40 acres & 2½ yds of flints from Tylers field to Slynes. Mr W. Hodgson had 3 bushels of wheat 11/3. Mr Miles fetched 1 Bullock & 4 sheep." (Beech Farm Diaries)

3rd 1886 "One of the little boys, Percy John Claringbold, age 5½ years, while going home from school this afternoon was run over by a bakers cart and died about twenty minutes after." (Kenley National School Log Book)

4th 1940 The Caterham and Warlingham Food Control Committee issued Certificate of Registration No.146 to The Canteen at 97, Croydon Road, Caterham, registering it as a Catering Establishment.

1989 There was a serious rail crash just outside Purley Station. Five people were killed and 94 injured.

5th 1235 "Grant of the gift made by Margaret daughter of William to the Hospital of St Thomas the Martyr of Acre in Culesdon and to the knightly brethren there of all her land in Culesdon with the houses, buildings, men and all that goes with them." (Calendar of Charter Rolls)

1855   The Hon. Sidney Roper Curzon "in the presence of a large assemblage of visitors, with the Clergy and many Ladies and Gentlemen of the vicinity "performed the ceremony of cutting the first sod of the Caterham Railway, near Burntwood Bridge.

1891   "Received the following letter: 'Kenley March 3rd 1891 Measles is becoming prevalent and I would advise the closing of the School, Yours truly E. Diver.' (Medical Officer of Health) Acting on the above the School was at once closed." (Kenley National School Log Book) (See 13th April 1891)

6th   1342   At Coulsdon manor court Thomas and Jane Brownyng were ordered to repair or rebuild the cottage on the heath, previously held by John Ingeram, which they now held "in bondage by the payment of ¾d for right of entry and the usual dues and services, within twelve months of entry, and thereafter to maintain it without waste or damage. He then did fealty for his cottage."

1809   In Coulsdon the burial took place of "Richard Elston, who accidently poisoned himself at Court Lodge, aged 27 years."

7th   1837   In Caterham the burial took place of "William Reynolds, killed by a tree falling on him as he was driving a waggon through Croydon. 39 years"

1912   "Barren strawberry in flower close to chalkpit on Halliloo Hills. In this chalkpit a beech tree has had the chalk excavated for several feet under its roots and here the tramp class of people find a splendid camping site as the impenetrable mass of lateral roots and soil form a perfect roof for shelter in wet weather. They have cut a small hole in the centre of this mass so that the smoke from their fire below can pass out as of that of a chimney." (Arthur Beadell's Nature Notes)

1922   *The Times* reported that Miss Evelyn Hamilton Gruner was awarded £1,750 damages, plus costs, against the directors of the South London Cinema Company. They had conspired to induce her to buy the loss-making Coulsdon Cinema at an exorbitant price (£3,500).

8th   1915   The Lord Lieutenant approved the amalgamation of the 11 Voluntary Training Corps in the Croydon Recruiting area into two battalions. The area extended from Norbury southwards to Dormansland and from Caterham westwards to Oxted. (See 20th Feb 1915 and 16th Dec 1917)

9th   1886   "44 children absent from School this afternoon, a few of them stayed away to attend the funeral of Percy Claringbold who was accidentally killed last week and the rest stayed away to go to a tea party this evening at 5 o'clock. This tea drinking has almost emptied the School on half-a-dozen occasions, although by leaving at the usual time for closing the children would have plenty of time to get to the party by 5 o'clock." (Kenley National School Log Book)

      1896 "Parish Election meeting at Chelsham. Went & they made me Chairman. A Poll demanded." (Beech Farm Diaries)

10th 1903 "Purchase of Angus Aberdeen Bull age 12 months: £13 2s 6d. G.W.R. Carriage of bull from Birmingham: 12s 3d." (Account Book of John Sherwill of Layfield Farm, Chipstead)

      1926 A Peal of Plain Bob Major was rung on the bells of St Nicholas' Church in Godstone, the 5,040 changes taking 2 hours and 39 minutes.

11th 1887 Kenley National School inspected: "General Remarks Boys & Mixed School: - This is a thoroughly good School. As the high mark was given in every subject, I may add that the examination in Religious Knowledge produced excellent results. The children were bright and answered with intelligence in both Bible and Prayer Book work - The Repetition included 9 Hymns, 2 Psalms, Scripture Texts, Miracles, Parables and a form of Private Prayers. The Church Seasons were thoroughly known, and the Paper work above the average met with in either town or country schools." (Extract from the report of the Inspector, Theodore Johnson)

12th 1962 The Farleigh Residents Association was formed with a total membership of 75. The main purpose of the association was to restore Farleigh to the Godstone Rural District (instead of to the London Borough of Croydon) "Since Farleigh is exclusively a rural and agricultural area, it has no place in an Urban District or London Borough."

13th 1327 13 years old Edmund de Passele of Alsted and his servant, John Wallet, were murdered in Coulsdon, probably at the instigation of his late father's wife, Margaret. She was tried and acquitted in 1331, by a Coulsdon jury, apparently with the assistance of bribery and corruption.

      1785 In Coulsdon, Benjamin, the son of Benjamin and Mary Tolbert, was baptised—"The Godfather by mistake gave the name William, which was intended for & given to the following infant." (The latter was William, son of John and Mary Harber.)

14th 1674 Sanderstead parish collected 7/5d for a brief for Nether Wallop in Hampshire.

      1935 The Regal Cinema in Purley was showing *Forgotten Men* (a War Documentary) and *Mr Cinders*, with Clifford Mollison and Zelma O'Neil. There was a continuous performance, the doors opening at 2 p.m.

15th 1760 William Budgen, a 27 years old Corporal in the Militia, was buried in Coulsdon.

      1930 Death at the age of 91 of William George Gardner, proprietor of the Pleasure Resort on Riddlesdown that had provided entertainment to tens of thousands of people, young and old, over a period of more than thirty years.

16th 1929 The Garden Village "Flag Drive gave us a very happy evening on March 16th. The experiment was a great success for, as team vied with team the fun increased throughout the evening. Congratulations to 'Captain' Bridger and his stalwarts in their victory, with 16 points." (Chelsham and Warlingham Parish Magazine)

17th 1964 At 3 p.m. the Lord Lieutenant of Surrey opened the Health Services Clinic and Central Library in Stafford Road, Caterham. After the ceremony guests were invited to view the Library and Clinic and to take tea in the Library with the Chairman of the County Council.

18th 1871 *The Croydon Advertiser* was "very pleased to refute a rumour that has prevailed in Caterham and the adjoining district for some time past 'that the small pox is very bad at Caterham.' We speak advisedly and from authority that a worse mistake was never made and that not a single case of small pox has shown itself in any family in Caterham.....A rumour like the above allowed to go unnoticed tends seriously to affect the tradesmen of the place as well as to keep away those persons who like a day's excursion to ramble amongst the Surrey Hills."

19th 1826 "I did not hear from Mr William today as he was busy pulling down the first part of old London Bridge." (Diary of Mrs William Jolliffe of Merstham)

1986 A grant was made from The Lloyds Bank Fund for Independent Archaeologists to the Bourne Society's Archaeological Group. The £50 cheque was presented at the Society of Antiquaries in London, and was used for the purchase of two new wheelbarrows.

20th 1905 The following children were sent home this morning - Lionel Bourne, Leonard Bourne, Elizabeth Bell and Rose Walker "with dirty heads" and Frank Waite "generally dirty - the latter two returned to school this afternoon and as nothing had been done to make them clean they were sent home again." (Maple Road Junior (Mixed) School Log Books, Whyteleafe)

1934 13 acres of land in Warlingham, which had formerly been part of Crewes Farm Estate, were sold for a development of 76 houses—"The Land lies well for building and is ripe for immediate development."

21st 1233 Henry III, in Croydon, ordered his treasurer, Peter de Rievaulx, to provide "Brother Roger, the hermit of Blecingele" with a quarter of wheat every eight weeks.

1944 "Caterham....another milestone in the life of the Regiment. Today came under the command of 107 AA Bde RA....and became the only Canadian Arty in the 21 Army Group under British Command." (War Diary 2nd Canadian H.A.A. Regiment)

22nd 1894 "I have lost two good girls this last week Rose Borer & Beatrice Southwood. The former was the most intelligent child in the School. At

Arithmetic I never had a cleverer scholar - a genius in fact. In addition to her work in this subject for Standard VII she has gone through most of the higher rules in Pendlebury's Arith. She is good in almost all her other work. Family arrangements have necessitated her leaving school sooner than we anticipated and it is with great regret I lose her. Beatrice Southwood is also a good girl, regular, neat, clean and painstaking. Her mother has called to explain why she has left the school and to thank me for the progress she has made. It is vexing to lose any of our intelligent regular Children - a few of the careless irregular ones might be better spared." (Kenley National School Log Book)

23rd 1892 "Fine Day but very cold. Men at plough and at flint cart. The thrashing machine here, thrashed out 48 qtrs of Oats; Paid Mr Brown on a/c £2. Rec'd from the Croydon Corporation on a/c of flints £51:17:6." (Beech Farm Diaries)

1918 The naval attack on Zeebrugge by H.M.S. *Vindictive* and her companion ships was commanded by Captain Alfred Francis Carpenter V.C., son of Captain Alfred Carpenter R.N., D.S.O., of Sanderstead.

24th 1632 In Sanderstead, Mary the daughter of Luke Clark, "a blind vagrant beggar", was baptized.

1944 'Little Selkirk', Caterham...."Tonight there is a heavy air raid. One house in our line suffers damage from an incendiary bomb. Some officers and men help extinguishing fires at Caterham." (War Diary 4th Medium Regiment R.C.A.)

1953 The Coulsdon and Purley Urban District Council was granted a coat of arms by the College of Arms.

25th 1739 In Warlingham "John the son of John Saxby and Mary his wife 'as she says' was baptiz'd."

1876 Mr Templeton of Old Lodge Farm in Coulsdon was offering for sale about 25 gallons of "Genuine Milk" daily at a price of One Shilling per Imperial Gallon, for cash only.

1928 The Electric railway service between London and Caterham and Tattenham Corner was inaugurated.

26th 1579 At the Kingston Assizes held today Peter Edmunds (or Edwards), a butcher from Westminster, was charged with grand larceny for having broken into the close of James Marden at Bletchingley and stolen three sheep worth 12s 8d belonging to John Saxbie, 4 sheep (16s 8d) belonging to Richard Saker and 6 sheep (24s) and a lamb (3s 4d) belonging to James Marden. He was found guilty but allowed clergy.

1886 "Whooping Cough has broken out in the Village & has reduced the average attendance very considerably this week especially in the Infant Room." (Kenley National School Log Book)

27th 1742   In Merstham parish 6s 8d was "Collected from House to House for the Sufferers by Fire at Marsh Gibbon in Com. Bucks. Loss £4,852."

       1965   The last of the old shops on the site of the new Hammond House development (in Croydon Road, Caterham Valley) to be demolished was No. 39, the jewellers, J.J. Browne & Son. It closed today at 5 p.m. A jeweller's shop had occupied the premises since before 1881. (See 29th March 1965)

28th 1871   "At 1 p.m., Mr Orchard and a boy in the employ of Mr Whiffen, baker, Caterham Valley, while slowly driving along the main road, near to the Blacksmith's Arms, Upper Caterham, came in collision with a pony and cart driven by a boy, and belonging to Mr Marchant, plumber, and so frightened the horse which is a spirited animal, that he literally jumped upon the back of the pony, and afterwards rushed madly along the road till it reached the shop of Mrs Balch, grocer, where it made a desperate leap into the shop window, causing a fearful crash and a considerable amount of damage, to the consternation of the persons inside the shop, especially to Mrs Balch, who has been very unwell for some time past. Luckily no one was hurt. The boy, seeing the danger, jumped off from behind the cart, but Mr Orchard kept his seat, and by so doing no doubt was the means of preventing the horse doing still further damage. It is astonishing, considering the casualty, that the man and horse sustained only a trifling injury." *(Croydon Advertiser)*

29th 1901   "This morning being bright, the upper division of school.....were taken for their first 'Spring Walk' to observe the signs of spring." The route was "up the bank, across Mr Miller's farm, on to the downs overlooking Kenley, thence back into the Godstone Road, school being reached at 12.15. A great deal of interest was evinced by the children, and the relaxed discipline seemed favourable to the formation of a more friendly unity among the children and gave me some insight to their characters." (Maple Road Junior (Mixed) School Look Book, Whyteleafe)

       1965   J.J. Browne & Son, the Caterham Valley jewellers, reopened for business at their new premises (No. 33, Croydon Road.) It was built on the site of the demolished Florida Cinema. (See 27th March 1965)

30th 1253   A grant was made to the Abbot of Waltham of "free Warren in his lands in Norfolk and Suffolk and Caterham in Surrey, provided the lands are not within the king's forest." (Calendar of Charter Rolls)

       1665   John Hayward was fined 20s for selling ale without a licence at Warlingham.

       1851   The census in Chelsham—which recorded 63 inhabited houses containing 171 females and 194 males—also reveals 4 males and 7 females, all shown as agricultural labourers born in Ireland, sleeping in barns in the parish.

31st 1811 Coulsdon Vestry gave Wm. Poplett "the sum of two pounds to gett two Bottles of the Birling Medicine he having being Bite by a Mad Dog & also Gave his Brother five shillings & 6d to go & fetch the same."

1878 Ann Hayes, a tramp, was caught in the premises of Mr George Parbury of Caterham. She was subsequently charged with being there for an unlawful purpose. She had previously been in prison over 40 times for drunkeness and disorderly conduct. She was sentenced to 14 days imprisonment and "on leaving the dock she remarked that she could sleep that term." *(Croydon Advertiser)*

1909 Princess Christian (fifth child of Queen Victoria, baptised Helena Augusta Victoria and married to Prince Christian of Schleswig-Holstein-Sonderburg-Augustenburg) opened Purley Cottage Hospital. She was President of the Royal British Nurses' Association and herself had a certificate for proficiency in nursing. The Purley contingent of the Territorials formed the Guard of Honour and an escort was provided by the Surrey Yeomanry and the Coulsdon District Boy Scouts. The Princess allowed the women's ward to bear her name in commemoration of the event and the Scouts to be called the "Princess Christian's Own Troop." *(Plate VI)*

APRIL

1st 1661 Thomas Rowett, Lawrence Rowett junior and John Rowett, all yeoman of Caterham, were charged at the Surrey Quarter Sessions with having, on this day, "made riot, battery, assault and affray there upon Marryan Francis."

1713 The baptism took place in Bletchingley church of General, son of Ralph and Anne Monk. The parents' politics are difficult to determine, as the General Monk was the most successful turncoat of the Civil War.

1871 About six acres of heather were destroyed when "some evil disposed person set fire to the heather which grows abundantly on Chaldon Common. The recent dry weather assisted their base intentions." Luckily, Police Constable Brooksbank perceived the outbreak and, with the help of Mr Chapman of the *Pitfield Arms* and several other men, extinguished the blaze. "The conflagration witnessed at a distance looked very grand....we sincerely hope the guilty party may be brought to justice as we are informed that this is the third time the heather on Chaldon Common has been set on fire." *(Croydon Advertiser)*

1974 Tandridge District Council came into being, taking its name from the Saxon Hundred, an administrative unit which encompassed much the same area a thousand years earlier.

2nd 1810 Thomas Durrant, a Merstham miller, won an action at the Kingston Assizes against quarry owners Jolliffe and Banks, for damages incurred by the failure of the mill stream precipitated by the completion of a drainage tunnel to lower the water level in the stone workings.

1886   "Whooping cough still very bad." (Kenley National School Log Book)

1934   Purley's second picture palace, the Astoria, opened. Calling itself "The Cinema Supreme" the main opening films were *The Way to Love* with Maurice Chevalier and *Ever in My Heart* with Barbara Stanwyck, plus a Laurel and Hardy short. Robin Richmond played the cinema organ. There was seating for 1,550 people. *(Plate VII)*

3rd   1889   Caterham Choral Society gave a performance of Gaul's *Joan of Arc* at the Lecture Hall in Harestone Valley. The price of admission was one shilling.

1992   The first day of a new venture for Bourne Society excursionists: a three day trip away. The places visited included Cirencester, Gloucester and the Forest of Dean, including parts of the extensive iron ore mines.

4th   1903   In Kenley the Regent St Polytechnic held an Exhibition of animated photographs under the chairmanship of Rev. H. Granville Dickson. "600 people were present from all parts of the parish.....through the kindness of Mr W. Webb about 40 girls and boys belonging to the Warehousemen, Clerks & Drapers' School witnessed the entertainment." *(Caterham Free Press)*

1944   Meetings of the St Nicholas Youth Fellowship usually took place in the C. of E. School in Godstone, from 7.30 to 9.30 p.m., but "As school was bombed Dancing in Barn (rent paid by Mrs Honeyman)." (S.N.Y.F. Minute Book)

5th   1912   "Great brownwinged orchid in bud on Leas. I kept this plant under observation for months, but it failed to flower as cattle or some person trod on it and retarded its growth. We were without rain for over a month so I carried water to it but without success." (Arthur Beadell's Nature Notes)

6th   1680   Richard Lewis, curate of Merstham recorded in the parish register a "Certificate to his Ma^{ty} about touching for ye Evill signed by ye Rector & Chierchwd. of Merstham." The eight names listed span 6½ years, the latest being "To Jane Buckner, spinster, April 6th 1680."

7th   1608   "We took iiij Rogues 2 men and ij women on Blyndlye heathe and had them to Godstone they had stolen ij duckes and accused eche other of other ffacts, and the 8th daye I went to Mr Evelyns and there we sawe them whipped and made them pasports to Devonshire and Somersetshire" i.e. where they came from. (Bostock Fuller J.P.)

1906   *The Purley, Oxted and Caterham Gazette* informed its readers of "A Transformation Scene" at Gardner's Pleasure Resort on Riddlesdown, where major redecoration had taken place and "the seating arrangements have undergone a complete change, the seats being made reversible. 500 visitors can now sit down to tea, whether it be wet or fine, and 600 can be comfortably accommodated at either concert, entertainment or dance." In total, the accommodation "enables over 2,000 people to be catered for at one time."

1915 Creation of the Urban District of Coulsdon and Purley. Previously the area had been part of the Rural District of Croydon.

8th 1670 Coulsdon manorial rolls record that "the Jury aforesaid say and present under this View of Frank-Pledge the Whipping Post for the correction of vagabonds and wanderers is missing by default of the inhabitants of Coulesdon whose duty it is both to provide and maintain it." They were given "until the feast of Pentecost next ensuing to set up the Whipping Post under pain of a forfeit to the Lord."

1912 "Saw the first swallow of the year near 'Upper Mayes'." (Arthur Beadell's Nature Notes)

9th 1647 At Warlingham manor court Helen Pace was fined 20s for "having William Levett as an illegal lodger for more than two months."

1912 "I discovered quite a new and interesting plant at the bottom of 'Highlane' called toothwort. It has the appearance of having grown in a dark place, such as a bluebell would look like if a pail had been turned bottom upwards over it during its period of growth, making the stem and flower a pale yellow." (Arthur Beadell's Nature Notes)

10th 1895 "The School broke up earlier by one day so that Mr & Mrs Smith"—the schoolmaster and his wife—"could take an excursion train to West of England - both in need of a rest & change of air & scene." (Kenley National School Log Book)

1944 "Godstone Y.F. went for a hike over Titsey Hill etc. Girls would have gone to Westerham, but boys could not stand it." (Minute Book of St. Nicholas Youth Fellowship, Godstone)

11th 1680 "Susan the daughter of John Austin (as & was alleadged) and Susan his wife was baptized at Chelsham Church."

1912 "On this date I was passing Hamsey Green Pond and made my first acquaintance of a pair of 'little owls', which were setting on one of the gray poplars near the pond. They were a little larger than song thrushes and spotted somewhat similar, only of course their heads were much larger. They were flying about as I watched. The daylight did not effect them like it does other owls which I have seen collide with branches of trees when disturbed in daytime from their roosting places." (Arthur Beadell's Nature Notes)

12th 1839 A Vestry meeting in Chipstead expressed its strong reactions to two Bills then before Parliament: "A Bill for further improving the Police in and near the Metropolis" and "A Bill for regulating the Police Courts in the Metropolis." They viewed the Bills with "great alarm and dissatisfaction" because of the "enormous and (as they conceive) most arbitrary and unconstitutional Powers thereby proposed to be conferred upon the Magistracy and Police depriving the people of their privilege of self-government and self-protection, destructive of the Rights and Liberties and comforts of the public."

13th 1891 The Medical Officer of Health, Dr E. Diver, gave permission for Kenley National School to be reopened (see 5th March). Children from 11 families were excluded for either one or two weeks more.

1962 *The Coulsdon and Purley Times* reported that "The East Surrey Conservatives and the Purley Young Conservatives have written to the council expressing 'concern' at the Library Committee's attempt to try and stop future meetings being held in the Purley Junior Library." They said that "if future lettings were ended they would have nowhere to hold their meetings as they did not have the capital to move elsewhere."

14th 1658 It was presented at the Court Leete of the manor of Limpsfield that "William West the elder gent. hath for a yeare last past and upwards harbored one William Morgan whoe is a Lewdfellow a common drunckard and a notorious swearer to the damage of the Inhabitants within the Jurisdiction of this Leet." William West was amerced 5s and ordered to remove William Morgan "out of this Leet before the feast day of John the Baptist now next coming upon paine to pay in default thereof 5s of Lawful money of England."

15th 1608 "I caused to stoute Rogues called Marye Rendall a wydow, and Anne Marks a wife to be whipped at Tanrydg and sent to Rowlyns in Essex." (Bostock Fuller J.P.)

1819 "Sir Robert and Lady Sheffield arrived. It was their first visit and the bells were to ring but the church steeple was in such a ruinous state they expected it to fall if they rang!" (Diary of Mrs William Jolliffe of Merstham)

16th 1892 "A wonderful snow storm - snow 7 inches thick buried the lambs & filled the road up. Wind north. Men carting flints & taking Hay for the sheep. Thawed a little." (Beech Farm Diaries)

1941 "H.E. bomb landed near top of TITSEY HILL 835745 on rd WARLINGHAM - OXTED at 2230 hrs demolishing an army lorry and killing seven Canadian soldiers." (War Diary 3rd Canadian Infantry Brigade)

1941 "From 2100 hrs to 0500hrs LONDON is subjected to a terrific air raid. Four to five hundred German bombers participated. It was called the biggest blitz so far. At CATERHAM we heard the continuous procession of the raiders, the formidable A.A. barrage bursting all over the sky. The sky over the London area was bright as day. Parachute flares by group of eight were seen at many places; many of them fell over CATERHAM, over our billets. H.E. bombs were dropped near and around our billetting area. The next day two aluminum containers of these flares, 3 feet long by 9 inches diameter were found near our Headquarters." (War Diary Royal 22e Regiment, C.A.S.F.)

17th 1349 A Writ of this date led 10 days later to an Inquiry at Lagham which found that "After the Black Death the mill of the manor of Marden was out of repair and had brought in nothing that year, as all who used to come to grind were dead." (Calendar of Inquisitions)

1908 Good Friday. *The Purley, Oxted and Caterham Gazette* reported a new attraction at Gardner's Pleasure Resort on Riddlesdown, viz. Barber's Bijou Cinematograph, admission one penny. (Local children of the time remember Mr Barber as "Raspberry", from the appearance of his nose.)

1941 Hubert E. Pounds recorded that "During the night of April 16-17, 1941, when a heavy attack by enemy aircraft on London was in progress, a high explosive bomb fell in Freelands Wood, Farleigh, within one hundred feet of a hollow oak in which was a brooding Tawny Owl. Despite this shock, which must have been pretty intense, apart from the previous loss of two of her three eggs due to bird-nesting boys, the stoic Owl succeeded in rearing one lusty youngster."

18th 1912 "Captured an adder as it was sunning itself by pinning its head down with a forked stick and having previously made a slip knot in my handkerchief, I passed it over the reptile's tail, along its body to its head with my disengaged hand, tightened up the knot, and released stick. I kept it at least two months. Finally accidentally allowed it to escape. Ugh!" (Arthur Beadell's Nature Notes)

19th 1849 The Westerham coach was buried in a snowdrift on Titsey Hill and had to be left there all night.

1912 "Barn owl nest and 3 eggs in elm pollard at 'Crewes Farm'." (Arthur Beadell's Nature Notes)

1941 A parachute mine dropped by a German aircraft on South Merstham killed five people waiting for a bus, destroyed half of All Saints' Church and demolished the vicarage, severely injuring the vicar and one of his two sisters and killing the other. (See 25th April 1943)

20th 1885 Kenley National School opened in the charge of Walter Smith. (The Log Book refers to it as 'Kenley C.of E. No. 1')

1891 "The children seemed very pleased School is opened again, and have commenced work in earnest. A good many seem weak after their long illness. Scarcely a child in the Parish seems to have escaped the complaint," (measles) "and there have been several deaths through it." (Kenley National School Log Book)

1941 In Caterham at "1600. Bde H.Q. Mess inaugurated weekly guest day. Lady friends were guests of some officers and tea was served. 2300 A near-midnight snack of Canadian corn, Canadian butter and Canadian Rye Crisps was enjoyed by several members of the Staff. Two members of the Staff liked bully beef." (War Diary 3rd Canadian Infantry Brigade)

21st 1556 A special commission at Southwark heard about a conspiracy formed against Mary Tudor and led by Richard Uvedale. A meeting had been held at Chelsham Court (Uvedale's house) "in treasonable consultation to steal treasure from the Exchequer and raise an army against the Queen."

1613 Three Indentures were signed whereby the three children of "one Sparke of Nutfield were bounde prentyses"—Thomas Sparke to John Gawton for 12 years, Eustace Sparke to Robert Killycke for 11 years and Jone Sparke to Tho. Darbye for 15 years. (Bostock Fuller J.P.)

1912 "I was pleased in that the nightingale, after an absence of 4 or 5 years has returned once more to its old quarters at Farleigh Hill. It was here it could always be heard first each year. Wild hops appearing at old hop garden near Crewes Wood." (Arthur Beadell's Nature Notes)

22nd 1438 At Merstham manor court "Robert Dawe brought a charge against John and Isabel Daly that Isabel had broken into his house at Merstham and had found string called 'Twyne' worth 6d and had stolen it causing damage of 3s 4d. John Daly declared that Isabel was not guilty and asked for a trial by jury."

1878 *The Croydon Advertiser* reported that William Burnell and George Gettings, both of Godstone, were summoned for selling underweight bread on this day to John Bates. They were fined £1 with 15s costs. On the same day George Harbour and James Gatwood, both of Warlingham, had been disorderly and refused to leave the *Railway Hotel* in Caterham, doing damage valued at 5s and assaulting the landlord and two policemen. They were sentenced to 14 months hard labour.

1886 "Whooping cough is still very bad in the parish, the attendance has been very low." (Kenley National School Log Book)

1941 "The Volley Ball Season was officially opened at Bde H.Q." (at 'Tinnivelli' in Caterham) "today. A team composed of 'Terror' Addie, 'Streak' Oxley, 'White Hope' Hay and 'Man Mountain' McAdam severely trounced one made up of 'Pretty Boy' de la Sabliere, 'Gorgeous' Johnson, 'Peaches' Bramfitt and 'Lullaby' Hamilton." (War Diary 3rd Canadian Infantry Brigade)

23rd 1727 Warlingham parish register expresses its doubts in Latin: "John the Son of Thos. Adlum (muliere si credas *) and of Sarah Matthews, a Traveller, was Baptized." (* i.e.'if you believe the woman').

1871 The son of Mr King, a Warlingham farmer, found "an innumerable quantity of feathers, sheep skins &c., &c." in the mouth of the nearby tunnel of the abandoned Surrey and Sussex Railway. "During the last few months several nocturnal visits have been made to the owners of fowls and ducks and in some cases as many as 20 fowls have been missed in one night. A fortnight since G.W. Woodroffe Esq., of The Salmons, lost a fine lamb and one of the skins found in the tunnel corresponds with the lamb lost." *(Croydon Advertiser)*

24th 1958 From 19th to 26th there was a week of celebrations to mark the opening of the Caterham Community Centre. On 24th the Caterham Community Choir gave a concert at 8 p.m., tickets 2/- and 1/-. The hall seated 250 people and was described as having the most efficient form of heating that could be found viz. "Electrical Night-Store Heaters" which kept the whole building at a constant temperature of 65 degrees Fahrenheit.

25th 1784 Bletchingley churchwarden's accounts record the payment of £1 18s 1½d to William Chillman for "Gazing at the Church." (Unfortunately this is probably a slip of the pen—Mr Chillman was a plumber and glazier, not the holder of what sounds like a plum job.) *(Plate VIII)*

1943 The bishop of Southwark consecrated the temporary church built by Canadian military engineers at South Merstham to replace the bombed All Saints. (See 19th April 1941) A new church was opened in 1952, and the temporary building, called Canada Hall, still serves as a parish hall.

26th 1575 A Probate Inventory was taken of all the "goodes and movables" of William Todhams deceased, of Horne, by John Winchester of Tanrygge and Robert Wyllat of Horne. The total valuation amounted to £22 2s 11d and his effects included 2 oxen (£5), 2 "ould mares" (£1 6s 8d), 3 stallions (£4), "1 acare and a halfe of wheat" (£1), "1 fether bead, 1 bolster, 1 coverlet, 1 blancet" (16s), "16 pieces of pewter, 4 porryngers" (18s), "6 candell styckes" (3s).

27th 1817 "In the morning Emily and myself watched the trees from France being planted in our garden. Kennedy, Lord Derby's gardener from the Oaks, assisted all day himself. The old apple tree by the greenhouse was cut down, and the people began moving earth for the alterations to our house." (Diary of Mrs William Jolliffe of Merstham)

1836 Mr Penfold put before the Croydon Vestry the Poor Law Commissioner's Warrant "forming a Union to be called the Croydon Union consisting of the several parishes of Croydon Addington

Coulsdon Sanderstead Woodmansterne Beddington with Wallington Mitcham Merton Morden and Penge Ville and directing the Election of Guardians to take place on the 21st of May next."

1947 What was probably the last aeroplane to fly from the private grass airfield at Hamsey Green (opened in 1933 and owned by Richard E. Gardner) took off today. It was a BAC Drone G-AEJS registered to the Drone Syndicate in 1946. It crashed at Gerrards Cross, badly injuring the pilot.

28th 1324 A Commission was held at Fulmer "concerning eight men, including the chaplain William de Welkested, who entered the park of Blechyngleye Surrey which is in the king's hands, hunted therein and carried away deer and assaulted John Bronnyng, the kings parker." (Calendar of Patent Rolls)

1459 At the manor Court of Chelsham Watevyles it was presented that Thomas Thornton had, every year for the past five years, broken into the lord's closes called Watevyles and Le Brome with his "oxen, cows, heifers, steers, horses, pigs and sheep" which had "grazed the lord's pasture there and consumed hay to the value of 40s and had trampled it down." He had also, over the same period and with his servants and dogs "secretly and wrongfully chased the lord's rabbits to the value of 40s. They killed them, took them, and carried them away." They were fined 22s.

29th 1460 At Farleigh manor court "Thomas Kempsall was fined 12d for breaking and entering the lord's rabbit warren and stealing twelve pairs of rabbits."

1804 Gilbert Buchanan, Rector of Woodmansterne, recorded in his parish registers that at the *Rose and Crown* in Kenley Mr Addington, a surgeon of the Royal Jennerian Society, inoculated nine poor children of the parish of Coulsdon with cowpox to protect them against smallpox.

30th 1866 Haydns' Dictionary of Dates mentions a "memorable railway accident" near Caterham Junction (i.e. Purley) on the London and Brighton line, in which three people were killed and twelve more injured.

1921 At the burial of Edmund Byron, lord of the manor of Coulsdon, at St John's Church, the funeral bell tolled 77 times—once for every year of his age.

1946 "We had exciting rounders in the field behind the Church, until Mr Cockram came along and told us in the politest language to 'GET OUT'. Did he swear??!" (Minute Book of the St Nicholas Youth Fellowship, Godstone)

MAY

1st 1661 At the Surrey Quarter Sessions Mary Rabett, widow, William Browne, cordwainer, and Thomas Staples, victualler, all of Caterham, were charged with each having kept a common Alehouse there without a licence since this date.

1791 The first journey of the Brighton Mail Coach was made. It was at first drawn by two horses, and the trip took twelve hours. (It travelled from London via Croydon, Purley, Godstone, East Grinstead, Lewes, and Newhaven to Brightelmstone.)

1912 "Carrion Crow nest and 3 eggs. This is our first record of a crows nest here. This one was found near the Asylum." (Arthur Beadell's Nature Notes)

2nd 1357 A letter written on 31st Jan 1781 and entered into the Coulsdon parish registers says that "Peter at Wode had Licence for another" (Chapel) "at his house at La Wode in Coulsdon" on this date.

1901 Horse trams commenced operating to Purley.

1928 Death of Henry Edward Kershaw who, in 1900, became the first Mayor of the Metropolitan Borough of Shoreditch. Between 1900 and 1907 the Kershaw family had lived at 'Viewfield' in Kenley. His son left a photographic record of the house and its splendid grounds in an album inscribed "E.M. Kershaw. An eight years memory of a happy boyhood." *(Plate IX)*

3rd 1197 Geoffrey de Titsey "for 10 marks granted to his kinsman William son of Odo de Titsey ½ hide at Chelsham and a virgate at Nettlestead, co. Kent, to hold from him at 7s rent."

1932 Warlingham Girl Guides held a concert in aid of Company Funds in the Church Hall. Among the displays was an ambulance display in which "First Aid was rendered most efficiently to a child knocked over by a bicycle and suffering from a compound fracture of the fibula and serious scalp wounds. She was most successfully treated and was carried away on an improvised stretcher, later being seen running about none the worse for her experiences." (Warlingham and Chelsham Parish Magazine)

4th 1543 In a Survey of the Manor of Caterham the tenants reported on oath that the vicar and his predecessors had always had a pension of £1 6s 8d a year "for an increase of his living."

1797 Merstham parish registers, in recording the burial of Sarah Weller who died on this day of a fever, aged 39, show her occupation as "Quarryman". (It is believed from other records that this should show "Henry" rather than proving the presence of women quarry-workers.)

Plate I (above)

Inside the Caterham and Warlingham Urban District Report and Control Centre

— see 16th January 1941

By direction of the National Council of Y.M.C.A.'s Incorporated

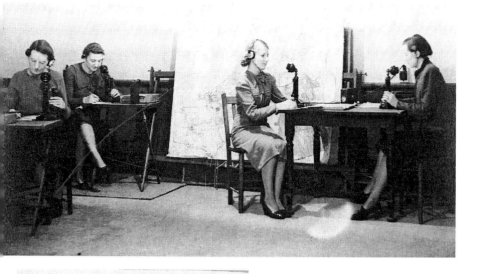

Y.M.C.A. HUT,

PURLEY.

On the Grounds of The E. Surrey Water Works.

CATALOGUE

OF

THE HUT

about 65 ft. x 30 ft. with additional Outbuildings as erected in Sections; also

The Contents

in Lots, including 2 Stoves, Striking Clock, the Apparatus of 2 W.C.'s, 2 Lavatory Basins,

18 COLLAPSIBLE TABLES 150 CHAIRS

10 FOLDING CARD TABLES.

a Caterer's Iron Boiler, about

250 YARDS OF LINOLEUM

and other effects, which

MACHIN and GRAHAM-KING

Have been instructed to Sell by Auction on the Premises

ON WEDNESDAY JAN. 23rd, 1924

At 2 o'clock precisely.

On view morning of Sale. Catalogues on application to the Auctioneers' Offices—

GODSTONE ROAD, PURLEY. (Telephone Purley 104).
BRIGHTON ROAD, COULSDON. (Telephone Purley 898).

CROYDON TIMES LIMITED, PRINTERS, 108, HIGH STREET, CROYDON.

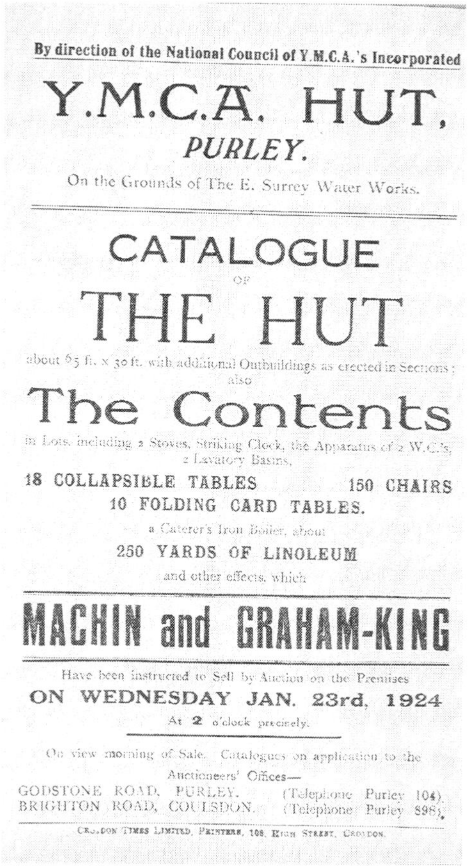

Plate II (left)

Front cover of Auctioneer's catalogue

— see 23rd January 1924

Plate III (right)

Front cover of programme of Annual Dinner and Smoking Concert

— see 25th January 1929

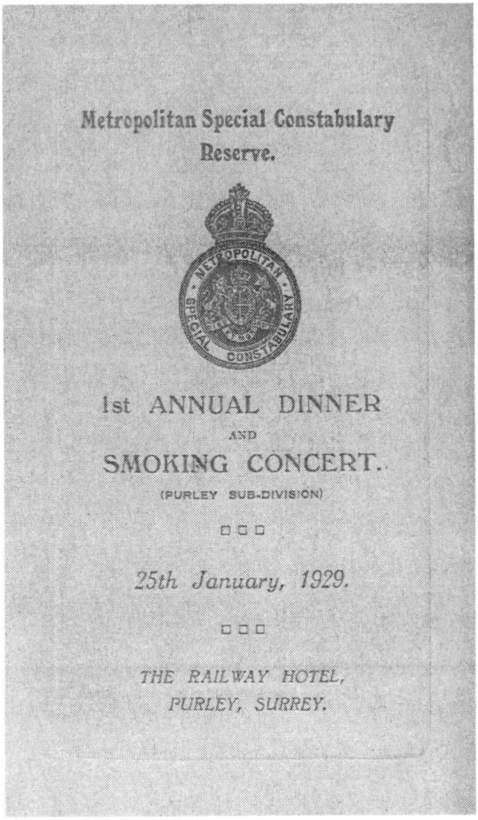

Metropolitan Special Constabulary Reserve.

1st ANNUAL DINNER
AND
SMOKING CONCERT.
(PURLEY SUB-DIVISION)

□ □ □

25th January, 1929.

□ □ □

*THE RAILWAY HOTEL,
PURLEY, SURREY.*

Plate IV (below)

Layfield Farm, Chipstead

— see 19th February 1903

Plate V

Beech Farm, Chelsham, home of Solomon Windross

— see 29th February 1892

Opening Ceremony, Purley Cottage Hospital, by Princess Christian, March 31st 1909.   copyright C.W.Burdekin.

Plate VI

Princess Christian opens Purley Cottage Hospital. The Scouts in the
picture formed part of her escort

— see 31st March 1909

Plate VII

The Astoria Cinema, Purley

— see 2nd April 1934

Plate VIII

Men at work on Bletchingley church. It looks harder than
"gazing" at it!

— see 25th April 1784

Plate IX

Inside *Viewfield* in Kenley early this century

— see 2nd May 1928

Plate X

Princess Christian pictured in her younger days

— see 2nd June 1903

Plate XI (right)

Entrance to Welcomes Farm, Kenley

— see 3rd June 1905

Reproduced by kind permission of Croydon Libraries, Museum & Arts

Plate XII (below)

Purley Fountain in the grounds of the East Surrey Water Company

— see 14th June 1983

Reproduced by kind permission of Croydon Libraries, Museum & Arts

Plate XIII (above)

Stone Age group at the Festival
of Britain Pageant in
Warlingham and Chelsham

— see 23rd June 1951

Plate XIV (right)

Front cover of Auctioneers
catalogue

— see 4th July 1917

COULSDON COTTAGE,
STOATS NEST ROAD, BRIGHTON ROAD,
COULSDON.

12 Minutes from Smitham Station and 15 Minutes from Purley Station and Tram Terminus. Reigate Motor Buses pass end of Road.

A CATALOGUE
of

90 HEAD OF POULTRY,

COMPRISING BLACK LEGHORNS, RHODE ISLAND REDS, WHITE LEGHORNS, BUFF ORPINGTONS AND CROSS BREEDS,

Also appliances, including

Show Hampers, Grit Boxes, Hen-coops, Grit Crushers and Mincer,

7 INCUBATORS,
by HEARSON, TAMLINS, PHIPPS and GLOUCESTER,

5 FOSTER MOTHERS,
BY WELL-KNOWN MAKERS,

WIRE NETTING, POLES, GALVANISED CORN BIN, LADDERS, GARDEN TOOLS;

15 FOWLHOUSES,
by LORD BROTHERS and OTHER EMINENT MAKERS,

An AIREDALE TERRIER, GREAT DANE PUP (10 months old),
and miscellaneous effects,
which will be sold by Auction by
MESSRS.

MACHIN & GRAHAM-KING
on

WEDNESDAY, JULY 4th, 1917
at **2.30** o'clock precisely.

ON VIEW MORNING OF SALE. Catalogues at place of Sale or at the Offices of the **GODSTONE ROAD, PURLEY** and Auctioneers. **Mr. H. B. BOND'S** Estate Office, **COULSDON STATION**

W. T. RAMSDEN, The Printing Works, Kenley.

5th   **1492**   At Merstham manor court Robert Killick was fined 4d because he "is a procurer and keeps a disorderly woman to the common nuisance." He was also fined 8d "for selling bad meat in the market - that is - one boar and pieces of pork - with the intent to deceive the local people." Also each of the following was fined 6d: William Punchon junior, William Punchon senior, John Alen, William Stone and Richard Tye because they "are vagabonds, and serve no man but live suspiciously."

6th   **1641**   A Bill required all Englishmen of 18 or more to take an oath to support etc. the "true Reformed Protestant Religion." In Chelsham, for example, 11 householders and 22 youths took the oath, with no-one refusing. There were very few in the area who did not take it and they are mostly shown as being absent at the time, one man in Titsey being away "serving His Majesty."

        1703   Bletchingley churchwardens collected 12s 8d for the "distressed Protestant Ministers in Hungary."

        1744   At a Vestry Meeting held in Merstham it was found that "an Evil Custom hath prevailed in this Parish of Spending the publick money. It is hereby ordered & enacted by the majority of a vestry ....that no Churchwardens for the future after this Date hereof shall allow above fifteen shillings to be paid for Ringing Viz: five shillings on the Nativity of our Saviour, five shillings on his Majesty's Birth Day and five shillings on Gunpowder Treason."

        1893   "Children who won RSPCA Essay prizes went to the Crystal Palace to receive prizes from Baroness Burdett Coutts & Lady Aberdare." (Kenley National School Log Book)

7th   **1892**   "AN EXTRAORDINARY EGG. Passers by Mr R. Warren's dairy shop, Colin House, Caterham Valley, have this week been attracted by a very large egg which was on view, weighing ¼lb all but ¼oz. The egg was a Caterham production." *(Caterham Free Press)*

        1945   "At 7.45 p.m. the news was given out that the next two days would be celebrated as Victory in Europe days. Within ¼ hr the bell-ringers were at the Church, and they rang for ½ hr." (Minute Book of the St Nicholas Youth Fellowship, Godstone)

8th   **1661**   William Sparrow of Limpsfield appeared at Surrey Quarter Sessions where he pleaded guilty to stealing a lamb worth 11d from Lady Mary Gresham. He was sentenced to be whipped.

        1893   "Pleasant surprise for Mr Smith. The girls who entered the RSPCA competition gave Smith a four bladed pocket knife." (Kenley National School Log Book)

        1920   The Peal Book of St Nicholas Church in Godstone records the first Peal on the new bells (see 16th Sept 1915). This was a Peal of Grandsire Triples, consisting of 5,040 changes which took 3 hours and 2 minutes.

1945 "Mr Stokes (A.R.P.) kindly gave us some thunder flashes and incendiary bombs to explode on the Green before and after a game of rounders." (Minute Book of St Nicholas Youth Fellowship, Godstone)

9th 1871 Following a report that on this day "a stranger went into the Commonwealth Tavern, Caterham Valley, and called for a pennyworth of gin" and then, when the landlord's daughter had left the bar for a moment, helped himself to the contents of the till, the *Croydon Advertiser* complained that "It is high time Caterham possessed a day policeman, so that the ratepayers may have what they pay for, viz 'police vigilance'."

1887 "Admitted Lucy Wakefield, Harriet, Norah & Bassie Burley, Emily & Joseph Smith, Ernest & Frederick Potter. Henry Cannings also returned to school after a long illness. So many new children coming in so near the examination are a great hindrance, but we are likely to get more as a lot of new houses have been put up this Spring. The want of another teacher is very much felt now and our work is done with considerable difficulty. Violet Thain the only eligible girl in the School for that purpose put on as monitress this morning." (Kenley National School Log Book)

10th 1622 Andrew Linckfeild, a Chaldon labourer, stole 14 sheep worth £8 8s and a ram worth 12s at St Saviour, Southwark. For this, and for the theft 10 days earlier of a brown-black gelding (£6) from Gabriel Aynescombe at Chaldon, he was sentenced, on 17th July at Croydon Assizes, to hang.

1980 At 10 a.m. the East Surrey Museum in Stafford Road, Caterham, was officially opened by the Chairman of Tandridge District Council, Councillor W.P.G. MacLachlan, accompanied by a party of invited guests. The door was opened to the public at 11.30 a.m.

11th 1907 "Purrs from Purley, by Persian" *(Croydon Advertiser)* reported "the Purley Horse Show, which master says was so great an intrinsic success that the weather had little or no influence over it. The rain might pour, and the mud might splash and the motor cars might stick - which they did - but there were the handsome horses, and the gallant contestants in the tournament, and the interested crowd of spectators all the same, and nothing - not even the downpour - could dampen the spirits and cool the ardour of the supporters of the first Purley Horse Show."

1943 "Marden Park is now at its best and a tremendous contrast with the first experience last December with rain and mud. The vehicle and gun stands are now complete and the road widened. At present a fence is being built to mark the boundary of the camp and the Estate." (War Diary 2nd Medium Regiment, R.C.A.)

12th 1553 Chipstead parish registers record the visit of King Edward VI's commissioners—Sir Thomas Cawarden, Nicholas Lygn and James Skinner—"for the sale of the church goodes jewelles and plate." An

Inventory was taken and included in the items listed that were "Receyved unto the Kynges use" were a chalice and "all th ornamentes." The total value was 24 shillings and 11 pence.

1984   A Families' Open Day was held at Caterham Barracks by the 1st Battalion of the Coldstream Guards. The entertainment included a Ceremonial Display, a Regimental Band Display and a re-enactment of the Siege of Sebastopol in the Crimean War.

13th   1294   Visit by King Edward I to Bletchingley. While staying there he signed two letters, one of which was to the Sheriff of York directing him to release a clergyman, who was accused of murder, arson and harbouring criminals, for trial at a church court rather than in the king's court.

1871   Under the heading "More Fowl Robberies" the *Croydon Advertiser* reported that "During the present week several gentlemen in and around Caterham have again lost a quantity of their poultry.....During the winter months scarcely a week passed but some case of fowl, and even pig and sheep stealing occurred, yet, not in one single instance has there been the slightest clue to any of the offenders."

14th   1797   Before about 10,000 spectators Daniel Mendoza defeated Bill Warr in a prize fight, held at Smitham Bottom, for the English championship.

1885   Kenley National School was visited by the Revd Canon Stewart who "examined the School in Reading, Writing and Arithmetic. 93 children were present at the examination. In Arithmetic out of all the children examined in Standards only seven did the number of sums correctly to qualify for a pass viz:- 2 correct out of 4, thus corroborating what has been written in the Log Book with regard to the backward state of Arithmetic."

15th   1754   John Borer, labourer, and Thomas Martin, servant, both of Caterham and John Chandler of Coulsdon "make Oath that they were the Identical Persons that took and apprehended Thomas Davies late Servant to Sir Kendrick Clayton Bart for Stealing one Grey Gelding....for which a Reward of ten Guineas was advertised for taking the same Person." (See 24th August 1753)

1820   Chaldon churchwardens paid Joseph Sharpe Apparitor, £1 0s 6d, which included payment of 3s 6d "Apparitor's Fee for Altering the Liturgy of the Church of England, on the Decease of his late Majesty", 4s 6d for "Proclamation and Prayer for his Majesty's Recovery from his late dangerous illness" and 2s 6d for "Proclamation for the punishment of Impiety and Vice."

16th   1742   In Merstham "A Brief was read for Holy Trinity Church at Guildford in Com. Surrey & on the Monday following was collected from House to House 3s 10d."

1752   In Chipstead, William son of William and Hannah Page was "half baptised", (i.e. he was baptised privately—probably at home—and hastily as he was not expected to survive. In fiction, at least, some did survive e.g. Oliver Twist: "'And now about business', said the beadle, taking out a leathern pocket-book. 'The child that was half-baptised Oliver Twist is nine year old to-day'."

1944   "Should have been sausage cooking on the common. N.B. TOO WET. School ready for use again" (see 4th April 1944) "so we had an evening of games, dancing & discussion about social." (Minute Book of St Nicholas Youth Fellowship, Godstone)

17th   1608   "We had a meeting at Godstone to perfect the accounts of the poore." (Bostock Fuller J.P.)

1939   Warlingham Methodist Church held a Celebration Re-union Day to commemorate one hundred years of Methodism in Warlingham.

18th   1811   George Grundell, age 21, a labourer at the Merstham limeworks, died in an accident with the steam engine there. This engine was used for winding loads of building stone out of the underground quarries up an inclined shaft.

1957   Purley and District Scouts held a Jubilee Pageant of Scouting at Rotary Field in Purley. The Pageant was in two parts: firstly 'Historical', depicting events such as the Stoats Nest Disaster (see 29th January 1910), the first Jamboree at Olympia in 1920 and the "Gang Show Born" in 1932, and secondly 'The Scout Method' which included "As a Cub" and "Becoming a Scout".

19th   1690   In Warlingham "Thomas ye son of Thom. & Elizab. Haward an abortive born & Christened & dyed May ye 19th 1690."

1806   The Chaldon churchwardens paid 5s 6d "for thanksgiving for Lord Nelson."

1883   The Lord Mayor, Lady Mayoress and officers of the Corporation of London arrived at Purley in a special train and set out in a colourful procession along bunting-decked roads to visit each of the four Coulsdon Commons, to mark the formal dedication of them as land reserved for the "recreation and enjoyment of the public." (see 5th Feb 1883)

20th   1758   The burial took place in Sanderstead of "Elizabeth Stagg, by Certificate or order from ye Coroner, having fallen into ye well at the Fox."

1918   The night of the 19th/20th saw the last air-raid on London of the First World War. The Purley searchlight was in operation three times between 11.55 p.m. and 1.45 a.m. The final All Clear came at 2 a.m. (By this time the light was fixed in a concrete base in Kingsdown Avenue. Originally it was mounted on the top deck of a tram based at the Purley Tram Depot.)

21st 1871 "A large number of fowls were stolen from the premises of Mr Edwards, Rook Farm, Chaldon." *(Croydon Advertiser)*

1916 600 members of the Surrey Volunteer Training Corps carried out field operations on Farthing Downs. They included signallers, cyclists, an ambulance section and the two battalions each had a Bugle Band. "With the day gloriously fine, and the undulating country looking its best, the Volunteers thoroughly enjoyed the operations."

22nd 1752 Richard, son of Thomas and Hannah Page, was half-baptised in Chipstead.

1760 A note in Caterham's parish register number IV says "bought this Book at London for a shilling and is to serve as a Register Book for Catterham Parish."

23rd 1900 "There never was such a day in Caterham" according to a Special Edition of *The Caterham Free Press*. "It was a day of Red, White and Blue" when Caterham opened Queen's Park "as a memorial to the long and conspicuous reign of Queen Victoria." It was also her 81st birthday, and to complete "a galaxy of notable circumstances" it was a celebration of the Relief of Mafeking.

1904 Whit Monday Bank Holiday. *The Purley, Oxted and Caterham Gazette* reported that "10 years ago one would never have dreamt that Purley would become so noted, but the scene on Monday, which almost battles description, shows to what an extent the popularity of Purley and the pretty districts surrounding it have become. Thousands of trippers from early morning thronged the tram-cars, taxing the capacity of the company to its utmost limit."

24th 1551 King Edward VI wrote in his own hand in his diary "A earthquake was at Croiden and Bllechingliee and in the most part of Surrey but no harme was done."

1814 John Glover, churchwarden of Chaldon, paid £1 7s 6d to T. Harding "Printer, Bookseller, Stationer, and Newsman" of Minerva Office, High Street, Croydon for the "Binding, Repairing and Lettering of the Chaldon Parish Bible."

25th 1551 Wriothesley's Chronicle puts King Edward's seismic upheaval a day later: there "was an earthquake in Surrey, at Godston, Brenchingley, Titsey, Rigate, Bedington, and Croydon, and a sixtene miles in length about twelve of the clocke in the forenoune, which lasted a quarter of an hower, so that the howses, hills, and all the earth shaked that the people were in great feare of God, but no hurt doune, praysed be God theirfore."

1912 "Near the Asylum I found a robins nest containing 3 robins & 2 cuckoos eggs. 5 eggs in all. A rare occurrence for 2 cuckoos eggs to be found in one nest." (Arthur Beadell's Nature Notes)

26th 1842 The railway from Redhill to Folkestone opened to the public, passing through a tunnel through Tilburstow Hill near Bletchingley. In the previous year, when under construction, this tunnel required the largest concentration of railway navvies in south east England. It was 1,324 yards long, with cuttings at either end, one of 1,300 and the other of 1,050 yards.

1923 In Lumberdine Wood "I saw a bright red object nestling mid a bed of blue forget-me-nots. On close inspection it proved to be a toy balloon with a post card attached stating would the finder send in the P.C. (which had a ½d stamp attached) to the Young Helpers League Aerial Competition Beckenham. It was dated May 26th and numbered 83. (83 pennies to pay excess postage!!)" (Arthur Beadell's Nature Notes)

1943 "Marden - Training is emphasizing physical training and hardening exercises. The use of the Tillingdown Range near Caterham has been arranged." (War Diary 2nd Medium Regiment R.C.A.)

27th 1818 "Mr William and his two sons on horseback, and Emily and myself in our carriage and four, went to the Racecourse at Epsom. On our return we found that Lord Coventry and his family had arrived. We had a party of twenty-two at dinner." (Diary of Mrs William Jolliffe of Merstham)

1967 The memorial unveiled today to the late Mr Tom Sherlock of Sanderstead, at Sanderstead Pond, incorporated the supply of water to the pond as required. It was financed by the Sanderstead Residents Association.

28th 1614 A Probate Inventory was made of "all and Singular the goods and chattles of Richard Wooddroffe alias Sharpe, late of Caterham, Blacksmithe, deceased." The total value of his estate was £26 17s 0d. Items included: "One table, 2 formes, one cupboard and two wheeles" (6s 8d); "One little furnace, 2 firkyns and other olde tubbs" (12s); "One Anfyll, one paire of bellows, two sledges, three naylinge hammers and some little old iron" (£1); "One lame nagge" (13s 4d); One stawlc of bees (3s 4d).

29th 1953 The closing date for two of Coulsdon Chamber of Commerce's Coronation week competitions—one for the Best Front Garden and the other for The Best Decorated House.

1965 A Peal of 5,040 Grandsire Triples was rung on Godstone church bells in 2 hours 51 minutes, to commemorate the 50th Anniversary of the recasting of the bells. (This was eleven minutes faster than the first peal on these bells—see 8th May 1920).

30th 1805 The body of Robert Rutter was "found in a Pond near Addington." This note accompanies an entry in the burial section of Sanderstead parish register which says "Robert Rutter, Clerk of this Parish, 14 years, left his house on Sunday the 19th December 1802 & has not been heard of since."

1903 Parts of Purley were flooded by a great storm; water flowed down Banstead Road and Russell Hill Road, made the Brighton Road impassable, and swamped the *Jolly Farmers* and the neighbouring coach-building shed. The course of the storm was eccentric—Croydon was badly hit, but little or nothing of it was seen in Coulsdon where, at Cane Hill Asylum, the cricket match that was in progress there was played out to a finish. *(The Croydon Guardian)*

1953 A Comic Cricket Match was played at Marlpit Lane Recreation Ground between the Coulsdon 'Coshers' and the Smitham 'Smashers'. The advertisement for the game stated "Expert Cricketers will be at a disadvantage. Come along and witness 'Cricket' played as never before. Fun, Thrills & Spills - No Holds Barred."

31st 1609 A Probate Inventory of "All the goodes and catells of John Pullinger of Blechingly late decseced" was taken. The total value was £27 4s 8d and included amongst other items were: "3 swine" (8s 8d); "2 ackres of barlie on the ground" (£1); "an carte, an paire of wheles with a Dunge carte" (5s); "1 new bill, 2 axes, 2 bills and all other his workinge toolles and oulde iron" (£3); "his raiment" (£1); "redi munie" (£1).

1911 In a violent thunderstorm over east Surrey three inches of rain fell at White Hill, Bletchingley. Three entrances to the old stone quarries along Rockshaw Road were washed open by the sudden inundation, giving temporary access to the mediaeval workings lost for centuries. Clear evidences of this flood may still be seen in the workings today.

1916 The Battle of Jutland: the tattered remains of the colours flown by Commodore Goodenough on his flagship, H.M.S. *Southampton,* now hang in Coulsdon church.

JUNE

1st 1692 In Warlingham "Dorathy ye Daughter of Robert & Elizabeth Simmons a Twin received Private Baptism." (i.e. a baptism performed somewhere other than in church, usually at home.) (See 5th June 1692)

1746 The Bletchingley bell-ringers were paid 5s "at rejoycing over ye rebels." (i.e. for the victory at Culloden.)

1800 Caterham parish register records that "James son of Richard Norris & Anne (late Anne Brown, spinster) born Feb 11 & priv. bap. Feb 23 in the parish of Rumbalds Wyke, Sussex, & being sent home by order of a magistrate, was received into this Church."

1911 Stoats Nest Railway Station was renamed Coulsdon and Smitham Downs (for Cane Hill).

    1919   The Sailors & Soldiers Recreation Rooms run voluntarily at 42 High Street, Croydon, by Miss Edith Carr and Miss Kathleen Taylor for 3¾ years, finally closed. They gave £22 of their surplus money to the Reedham Orphanage in Purley.

2nd   1680   "The corpse of William Taplin was buried in the churchyard of the parish of Farley" under the terms of the Woollen Act. (See 8th June 1680)

    1903   Caterham's "memorial to Victoria the Good"—the new Caterham Cottage Hospital—was opened by Princess Christian "amid the fervent rejoicing of the whole neighbourhood." *(Caterham Weekly Press and County Post)* *(Plate X)*

3rd   1905   "Purrs from Purley, by Persian" *(Croydon Advertiser)*—"This has been a sporting week, and Master Jack has had his full, albeit somewhat chequered, share of what has been going on. There have been some interesting doings at Welcomes Farm, Kenley, where horses are put through their paces; the annual sports have been held at the Falconbury School on Peaks Hill, and there has also been some racing at a place called Epsom Downs." *(Plate XI)*

4th   1613   "Amias Gullock brought to me by the offycers of Gatton for stealing of a petycote which was taken with him; but the partie would not accuse him of ffelonye, and he said he boughte it. I caused him to be whipte and sent to the place of his byrth at Combe by Charde in Somersetshire." (Bostock Fuller J.P.)

    1808   The turnpike road from Foxley Hatch (Purley) to Reigate was opened despite much opposition from the rival Sutton and Reigate Trust, who favoured their own route and had delayed the passing of the Croydon and Reigate Turnpike Trust Bill in Parliament since 1796. The Croydon and Reigate Trust had to pay Sutton and Reigate £200 p.a. to compensate them for loss of tolls.

5th   1665   "John Taxe was sworne parrish Register for the parrish of Saunderstead in this County according to a late Act of Parliament entituled an Act touching Marriage & the Registering thereof and allso touching Births & Burials."

    1692   In Warlingham "Dorathy Simmons was buried in Woolen only" and "Sarah ye other Twinn was Baptized." (See 1st June 1692)

    1895   There was controversy after Warlingham Cricket Club played Godstone in the first match in the Village Cup Competition. The Warlingham and Chelsham Parish Magazine reported that Warlingham had won by one run but that the "Godstone scorer failed to enter one run to Baker in the second innings, and so claimed it as a tie. The run was actually entered in the Godstone book, but the scorer afterwards claimed that it was entered under protest."

1903   It was reported at the Godstone Board of Guardians that the workhouse held 133 inmates in the previous week, two less than the corresponding week the year before. The Infirmary housed 56 (51 the previous year). "The number of vagrants for the fortnight was 103."

1936   Official opening of Selsdon Wood Nature Reserve and Bird Sanctuary, by the Right Hon. The Lord Mayor of London (Alderman Sir Percy Vincent Kt.)

6th   1730   "On Saturday evening last a Cart going from Croydon Market to Godstone, in which were Mrs. Moor the Owner, the Widow Roffey of Coulston, and Mr. Causton's Daughter of Croydon, of about 12 or 13 years old, was overturn'd on Ricklesdown, about 4 miles beyond Croydon, and being loaded with Goods, and tilted, they were all smother'd to Death before they cou'd be got out. Mrs. Moor's Son drove the Cart. Mrs. Roffey has left 3 Children." *(Fog's Weekly Journal)*

1953   The closing date for more of the Coulsdon Chamber of Commerce's Coronation week competitions: the Word-Making, Window Display Judging, Misplaced Articles and Programme Printers' Error Competitions.

1991   *The Daily Mail* reported on the results of the analysis of bones excavated from a rubbish pit on the Tudor site at Little Pickle in Bletchingley (although the paper called it "a rubbish pit near Reigate"): "As well as vast quantities of venison, beef, mutton, pork, rabbit and duck, the menus included geese, woodcock, pigeon, snipe, quail, lapwing, golden plover and magpie. And fish dishes contained pike, herring, haddock, plaice, eel, cod, ling, sturgeon, carp and conger eel."

7th   1958   Among the prizes offered to the Carnival Queen at the Caterham and Warlingham Carnival were a year's free pass to the Florida Cinema, a permanent wave, a fashion voucher and many other gifts presented by local traders.

1986   The Lord Mayor of London, Sir Allan Davis, joined by the Mayor of Croydon, Peter Macdonald, and by the Southern Regional Director of the National Trust, David Musson, planted three oak trees in Selsdon Woods Nature Reserve to celebrate the 50th anniversary of the official opening of the Reserve on 5th June 1936.

8th   1552   Anne of Cleves wrote to Princess (later Queen) Mary Tudor from her house in Bletchingley asking for help with her financial affairs.

1680   Sir William Hoskins certified that the necessary affidavit was brought to him regarding the burial in Farleigh of William Taplin (see 2nd June 1680) confirming that he "was not buried in any shirt, shift, sheet or shroud, made or mingled with any flax, hemp, silk, haire, gold or silver, neither put in any coffin lined or faced with any thing."

9th 1788 The Prince Regent watched 'Gentleman' Jackson, 19, win his first prize fight, against William Fewtrell, at "Smith-in-theBottom". The contest lasted 67 minutes. The Prince awarded a banknote to the winner, who later went on to become champion of England as well as the landlord of the *Cock Hotel* in Sutton.

1945 "The Social on June 9th was very successful. Several parents & friends came. Dancing was the main item; but a few games were played. 'Bigamy' proved very popular." (Minute Book of St Nicholas Youth Fellowship, Godstone)

10th 1734 A letter (copied into the parish register) was written to the Merstham churchwardens reminding them of their duties following "a dispute among the people about their Seats and Pews" in the church. It told them to "take immediate Care that those Farmers who pay to Church & poor may have the quiet & peaceable possession of the several Seats & pews in the Church, of Right belonging to their respective Farms; that the people may be duley accomodated, without any illegal additions or alterations whatsoever, either in the Church or Chancel and without any Unnecessary new Charges upon this poor parish, there being to our certain knowledge still room enough and to spare for all the Congregation." Anyone who "would pretend hereafter to give any farther Trouble, should do it at their peril....Geo Cummings Curat."

1914 A Garden Fete and Sale of Work was held at Godstone Rectory with the aim of raising £200 for the restoration of the bells and bell-frame in St Nicholas Church. Over £500 was actually raised, enabling all six bells to be recast and a new treble and a tenor to be added to complete the octave.

11th 1953 As part of Coulsdon's Coronation Week celebrations Marks the Tobacconist, in Brighton Road, ran a competition open to anyone spending five shillings or more. Competitors had to forecast the number of runs to be scored in the England versus Australia Test Match which began on this day. The nearest forecaster would win a "Ronson Coronation Lighter."

12th 1360 At Westminster, Edward III granted "Pardon to Peter de Northeye in the company of Michael de Poynges for the death of Nicholas Colleville of Caterham." (Calendar of Patent Rolls)

1893 The Warlingham and Chelsham Parish Magazine reported some "very bad luck" in a cricket match Warlingham played against Bletchingley. "One man, who subsequently scored just the number of runs by which we lost, was run out; but the bails being off when the wicket was put down, the decision was, of course, in his favour. Just after this he was bowled, but the bail, though displaced, remained wedged between the two stumps, and did not fall to the ground. We have never heard of this happening before."

1988   The Dutch 'John Tomes Society' visited the East Surrey Museum and then Caterham cemetery, where Sir John Tomes and his wife are buried. A dentist, he "made probably the most significant contribution to the dental profession in the 19th century. He was one of the active voices behind the 1878 Dentists' Act, and was a founder member of the Association and its first President." He also "wrote the famous article 'On the Presence of Fibrils of Soft Tissue in the Dentinal Tubes'" in 1865. He was perhaps best known for introducing the first forceps to accurately fit the shape of the tooth to be extracted. *(BDA News)*

13th 1871   Two silver watches were stolen from a bedroom drawer at the *Royal Oak Inn* in Upper Caterham. Mrs Faulkner, the landlord's wife, "had been busily engaged during the whole of the day, preparing for a cricket supper, which, no doubt, gave the thief a better opportunity of carrying out his purpose. What makes the loss greater, one of the watches was a keepsake from a brother, who lost his life in the ill-fated vessel *The Captain*. It is needless to say the rogue got free." *(Croydon Advertiser)*

1891   St Mary's Church in Caterham reopened after a week's closure during which the whole building had been re-seated and part of it re-tiled. For the first time, the worshippers were summoned by a peal of bells. (These tubular bells were replaced in 1993 by the present bells).

14th 1969   Caterham Carnival Fete was held at Westway Common, Caterham Hill. All proceeds were to go to provide Medical Aid Equipment for the local Loan and Home Service of the British Red Cross.

1983   R. Mansell Ltd issued a Press Release concerning a "New Home for Purley Fountain", which was to be moved from its site in the East Surrey Water Works to the grounds of Purley Library, where it would "be back on public view by August this year, after almost a quarter of a century in hiding." The scheme was master-minded by Purley Rotary Club, and "Mansell, who are celebrating their own 75th anniversary" donated £500 towards the removal fund. *(Plate XII)*

15th 1912   "Birdsfoot and creeping yellow cress in flower. Birdsfoot is a rare plant local to Worms Heath. The seedpods are in shape like that of a birds foot. The creeping yellow cress I found near Kingswood Lodge on the right hand of bridle way to Farleigh Common, the only spot in the district." (Arthur Beadell's Nature Notes)

16th 1854   The Royal Assent was received for the Act of Incorporation for the Caterham Railway, with the provision that the line was to be completed within three years.

1917   On an outing of the Botanical Committee of the Croydon Natural History and Scientific Society to Farthing Down so many specimens of the Fly Orchis were found that one of the party "by standing on a certain spot and turning round, was able with a walking-stick to touch twenty specimens without moving from the spot."

1944   "First appearance of the German pilotless rocket glider in this area today. In all about a dozen came over this way, the first one crashing about 0810 hrs in Caterham-on-the-Hill." (War Diary 2nd Canadian A.G.R.A. at Moyle House, Caterham)

1944   "Everybody is quite interested by those German Radio control Planes. We see several of them. As long as we hear them, O.K. - it is when the engine stops running!! A few seconds elapse and BANG!!! It explodes." (War Diary 4th Medium Regiment R.C.A. at Little Selkirk in Caterham)

17th 1237   Henry III made a special grant of money for the care of the young Richard de Clare, who was ill at Bletchingley.

1803   Chaldon's Churchwardens and Overseers of the Poor were ordered by his Majesty's Deputy Lieutenants and Justices of the Peace for the Eastern Division of the County of Surrey to pay £4 4s to Henry Roffey who, after being chosen by Lot, had been serving in the Surrey Militia for a month. As his personal assets were under £500 he was entitled to half the price paid to a Volunteer. (There was a fine of £10 payable by the Overseers if they failed to pay this sum out of the Poor Rate.)

1944   "In the evening B.S.M. Laporte, 58 Bty, is slightly wounded by a tracer from a browning M.G." (i.e. Machine Gun) "firing at one of the pilotless planes. He stays with the unit as he will be cured shortly." (War Diary 4th Medium Regiment R.C.A. at Little Selkirk in Caterham)

18th 1544   A Grant was made to Sir John Gresham of "the manor and rectory of Warlingham, chapel of Chelsham and advowson of the vicarage of Warlingham. At 40s 10½d." (Letters and Papers Foreign and Domestic)

1866   The Prince of Wales opened the Warehousemen and Clerks' School in Purley.

1897   "Next week being Jubilee week - a weeks holiday is given. Before breaking up the National Anthem was sung, & a short address given to the children." (Kenley National School Log Book)

1983   The White House Club—Warlingham's Nudist Colony—held its Jubilee Ball, from 8 p.m. to 1 a.m., with the theme of "The Thirties."

19th 1942   "Today is moving day" (from Burton Rough to Caterham) "- it was a good move, everything proceeded according to plan, except that we arrived about half an hour early. The luxury after Burton Rough was rather staggering - but it will not be difficult to take." (War Diary 1st Medium Regiment R.C.A.)

20th 1608 A warrant was issued for "Tom of Godstone for taking a hatband from one of John Brookes men of Oxsted where the seyd Tom then dwelt which hatband he layed to pawne at Wyllyam Myles of Blechinglye, the plaintiff being here sayd he would not pursue yt as ffelonye and Myles gave him his hatband and therefore did not proceed in the matter." (Bostock Fuller J.P.)

1944 The king approved the posthumous award of the Victoria Cross to L/Cpl John Pennington Harman of the Royal West Kent Regiment, for his bravery when he was killed fighting the Japanese in Burma. He was the son of Martin Coles Harman of Chaldon. (See 16th Nov 1947 and 5th Dec 1954)

21st 1887 To start Caterham's celebrations of Queen Victoria's Golden Jubilee a programme of "Old English Sports" was held in the field behind the Post Office in Caterham Valley, by kind permission of C. Asprey Esq. Mrs Soper of Harestone distributed the prizes.

1897 Caterham began six days of celebration of Queen Victoria's Diamond Jubilee. It started at 3 p.m. with a Children's Entertainment and Sports and Games, followed by a march to the Public Hall and St John's School for Tea at 5 p.m., when each child was presented with a Jubilee Mug as a souvenir. Each school was presented with a Union Jack and, on returning from tea, the flags were hoisted on poles erected in the school grounds.

1939 Hamsey Green and District Residents' Association held a dance at the Church Hall in Warlingham in aid of the Children's Sports Day which was due to take place on 22nd July.

22nd 1895 "Damp morning, nice showers. Dulake finished cutting all grass etc this season. The others Horse hoeing mangold & swedes in the morning, carting Hay from Waterfield in the afternoon. Rec'd cheque from Fairfoot & Rooke for Income tax overpaid £3.5s.0." (Beech Farm Diaries)

1944 "Capt. Carroll gave a gas lecture to O.Rs. All Ranks getting hair cut to 1½" today." (War Diary 2nd Canadian A.G.R.A at Moyle House, Caterham)

23rd 1897 "A treat provided by subscription to all children in the parish of Coulsdon between the ages of 3 & 15. The children from Kenley Parish above the age of 6 met at the Nat. School at 2 p.m. & then marched in procession to Mr Gardner's Tea Gardens, where they met the children from Coulsdon, Cane Hill & Reedham. The children under the age of 6 were entertained in their various parishes. Those from Kenley at the Kenley Vicarage." (Kenley National School Log Book)

1944 "In the evening, one P-Plane is caught in the balloons which stand at around 3 miles in front of our mess and crash. The C.O. noticing that the balloon is busted, intends to find it and keep it. The balloon is found allright at around 6 miles from our camp, but the R.A.F. is already taking care of it, and the C.O. cannot get it." (War Diary 4th Medium Regiment R.C.A. at Little Selkirk in Caterham)

1951 A Festival of Britain Pageant was held in Warlingham and Chelsham, with various groups depicting local historical events e.g. "A.D.1086 Richard Chelsham and his seven Bondsmen - Warlingham & District Horse Club" and "1556 Arrest of Richard Uvedale at Chelsham Court - Wesleyan Youth Club." *(Plate XIII)*

24th 1871 Caterham residents who took "pains in cultivating their gardens" were frequently finding "in the morning their crops galloped over and their gardens trampled upon by stray horses from the neighbouring common. Surely if the owners of the horses are allowed to graze their horses free of expense they ought to use all possible means to prevent their straying and injuring property not exclusively belonging to the rich, but more especially to those who have to obtain their living by the sweat of their brow. At present Caterham Valley does not possess a pound or we would venture to predict, if it did, in a week hence from this time the different animals impounded therein would supply an interesting subject for any Zoologist." *(Croydon Advertiser)*

1943 "Authority granted to commence work on assault course near WARLINGHAM M.R.780764. Cpls McCaig W.J. and Atkinson C.R. made the recce and will construct the course." (War Diary 1st Battalion Royal Canadian Engineers, in Caterham)

25th 1940 "Attendance low this morning 107 present (50.7%) due to early morning Air Raid warning. Head teacher attended Roke School pm until 5 o'clock to await information re Medical Examination of children for Overseas evacuation scheme." (Kenley Junior Mixed and Infants School Log Book)

1983 A Bourne Society Car Ramble toured local churches in their pursuit of 'Church Symbolism', led by Mr Charles Pringle. They viewed the mediaeval wall painting of the Descent into Purgatory, the Harrowing of Hell, the Weighing of Souls etc. in Chaldon; the plain tomb of Sir Thomas Cawarden and "the heavily ornate, early Georgian memorial to Sir Robert Clayton" in Bletchingley; nothing at all inside Burstow church due to a wedding taking place; the Saxon nave at Worth and more wall paintings at Charlwood.

26th 1487 John Drewe of Farleigh wrote his Will and among other bequests were £3 6s 8d. for "the peyntyng of our lady in the parish church of ffarlegh" and "to Johan my wif vi akers of whete and xiii acres of otes....to John my brother ii acres otes and vi female shepe....to Alson my sister ii female shepe called youes....I bequeth my lammys to the disposycion of

John Drew my fader." (Parish Notes in Warlingham and Chelsham Parish Magazine)

1762   The first record of an organised match played by the Coulsdon Cricket Club appeared in the *Daily Advertiser* on this date. They played the Mitcham Young Club on Mitcham Common, at the "Sign of the Goat." (Mitcham won by 4 wickets.)

27th 1502   Margery Hextall was appointed by Edward, Duke of Buckingham, to look after his children at his "manner of Blechinglighe" during his absence. She was to have 17 servants to assist her and was to ensure that the children "be daylie served with foure or fyve dysshes of such flesh or fishe as....shall be thought convenient for the season of the yeare."

1871   "Caterham was all alive by the juveniles here ranging in age from ten to fourteen years, making preparations to start for Godstone to play a match with the young Godstonites on Godstone Green, for a supper consisting of bread and cheese and ginger beer. The match was superintended by Mr Edgar, of Godstone, and resulted in the defeat of the young Caterhamites by 11 runs, Godstone scoring 106 and Caterham 95. The boys here have a great friend in Mr Pash junior, who has spent lately a considerable sum of money in purchasing bats, balls &c for their amusement, and that gentleman's kindness is held in high esteem by the boys." *(Croydon Advertiser)*

28th 1780   Michael Wood and Edward Leigh, the Assessors, approved, signed and sealed the Land Tax of Chelsham compiled on 13th June. Twenty nine properties were assessed for a total sum of £91 5s 0d. The highest assessment was for £21 9s 4d on Chelsham Court, owned by Atwood Wigsell Esq. and occupied by Michael Wood, who had leased it since 1774.

29th 1942   An Inventory of the property of Frederick Charles Fuller at Halliloo, Warren Barn, Bug Hill, Chelsham Place and Slynes Oak Farms was made by Fox and Manwaring, Surveyors and Valuers. His livestock consisted of 169 cattle valued at £4,091 and 13 horses (Rosie, Tommy, Daisy, Ruben, Floss, London, Flower, Tinker, Nobby, Hector, Polly, Prince and Bill) worth £600. Among the dead stock were 6 x 10 gallon Milk Churns, a 1924 Terraplane Saloon Car, 24 Hay Forks and 6 Nosebags. The total valuation amounted to £8,670 7s 4d.

30th 1786   Coulsdon parish registers record "Received the favour of this further" (see 31st January 1781) "intelligence from Mr Manning at Godalming." The information supplied concerns the details of various records of the ownership of the manor of Watendon up to the time of King Edward VI.

1945   Members of the St Nicholas Youth Fellowship, Godstone, "went to see the Oxford Street Aircraft Exhibition, and in the evening formed part of the 'applause' for the B.B.C. programme 'Transatlantic Call, People to People', relayed from a converted cinema."

JULY

1st   **1540**   Thomas Wriothesley wrote to Henry VIII to tell him how Anne of Cleves had reacted to the king's letter detailing the terms of the divorce settlement, part of which was that she was to receive the manor of Bletchingley with its splendid house and parks. After her interpreter had explained the document to her, her immediate response was that she "demanded where Bletchingley was?"

        1891   A Programme of Sports took place on Godstone Green. Among the "Prizes to be competed for by those who Dine" were 2s for Throwing the 56lb weight, 1s for two Egg-and-Spoon Races, 2s for winning and 1s for second place in a Race for Men over 40—and no person was "to take more than 3 prizes."

2nd   **1278**   The expenses of lord William de Chelesham and his bailifff, William de Syleby, for the eight day period ending today, while at Farleigh, amounted to 21d for ale, 9¼d for meat and 4½d for fish.

        1872   The Caterham Churchwardens' Accounts record a meeting held to consider the question of burial in the Parish Church Yard of deceased inmates of the Caterham Asylum.

3rd   **1659**   The Council of State, hearing that the enemy (i.e. the Royalists) intended to meet at Redhill, ordered Major Audeley (see 16th August 1650) of Sanderstead to take his troops to Redhill before daybreak to arrest all suspicious persons found there and take their horses and arms. (Audeley lived at 'West Purley' the chief house in Sanderstead, later called 'Purley Place House' and then 'Purley Bury House.')

4th   **1917**   Machin and Graham-King held an auction at Coulsdon Cottage in Stoats Nest Road of 90 head of poultry (Black Leghorns, Rhode Island Reds, White Leghorns, Buff Orpingtons and Cross Breeds.) Also for sale were 7 Incubators, 5 Foster Mothers (by well-known makers), 15 Fowlhouses, an Airedale Terrier and a Great Dane Pup (10 months old.) *(Plate XIV)*

5th   **1333**   The manorial accounts of Farleigh for the period from 3rd May to this day show that the manor-house dairy produced one cheese every day. These were sold at prices ranging from 2d to 4d each depending on size. (At other times of the year cheese was made on alternate days. Generally milk from both sheep and cows was used, but in 1356 there was no sheep's milk because of an outbreak of a disease called "le Pockes.")

        1894   "Beautiful day, very warm. Fire broke out in our Barn burnt all the corn and straw & cow sheds etc. A dreadful time." (Beech Farm Diaries)

        1932   An agreement concerning the purchase of land at Tillingdown Lane in Caterham stipulated that it was to be used only for private residences costing no less than £500 each and that no part of the land was to be used, at any time, for the purposes of a Golf Club or Links.

6th   1893   The Royal Wedding Day (the marriage of Princess Victoria Mary (May) of Teck and the Duke of York) was heartily celebrated in Warlingham and Chelsham. Both parishes held cricket matches - in Warlingham it "was a cricket match with broomsticks, seventeen on each side, between Married and Single" (the Single men won easily, but were then defeated by the Married men in a tug-of-war) and in Chelsham a game between boys and girls "the result of which, perhaps the girls might not like us to set down." (Warlingham and Chelsham Parish Magazine)

        1894   "Very hot day. Thunder & rain in the evening. Very heavy storm. Dulake cutting carted Hay in Paddock. Farm buildings a wreck. Barn & Granary gone. Thankful no animals were burnt." (Beech Farm Diaries)

7th   1450   Pardons were issued to many involved in Jack Cade's rebellion, including Thomas Basset the elder, Thomas Basset the younger and John Basset, all "yomen" of "Cullesdon, co. Surrey, and all other men in that town" and "William Wodden of Warlyngham, John Wodden of Chelsham, John Planesfeld of Warlyngham and Thomas Thordon, John Thorndon, Richard Fythyan, John Blakbourne and John Virgely, all of Chelsham, and John Volantyne, Laurence Wanegate, William Maye and Thomas Knot all of Warlyngham, co. Surrey." Also "John Janyn of Croydon, co. Surrey, yoman, and Richard Rokenham of Collesdon, co. Surrey, yoman, constables of Walyngton hundred, and all in that hundred." Also "Richard Lynde, gentilman, John his son, William Lynde, William Ounestede, John Whyte and Robert Brook all of Sanderstede, co. Surrey."

        1894   "Fine day after the storm....The Insurance Officer came & made an offer of which I accepted & signed." (The offer was for £220.) (Beech Farm Diaries)

        1913   Caterham Valley's first Cinema opened to the rear of *The Commonwealth* public house. (It underwent restoration in 1923 and closed in 1928 when the purpose-built Capitol Cinema opened. See 6th October 1928)

        1944   "At 11 o'clock 50+ panes of glass broken by blast from Flying bomb. Attendance for week 35.7%." (Kenley Primary School Log Book)

        1986   B.B.C. Radio 4 broadcast "Church Bells on Sunday" live from St Nicholas Church, Godstone.

8th   1648   Major Audeley of Purley Place House reported to General Fairfax that he had pursued, fought and routed the new insurgent (i.e. Royalist) army in Surrey. (Calendar of State Papers)

        1802   Between 8th July and 29th six out of eight burials in Chipstead churchyard were of those who "died of scarlet fever."

        1944   "Saturday, school open from 10 a.m. to 3 p.m. for Evacuation Registration." (Kenley Primary School Log Book)

9th 1905 At 11 a.m. the Ancient Order of Foresters held a parade at St Mary's Church in Caterham, followed three days later by their Annual Dinner and Fete which was enjoyed "not least of all by the clergy present."

1984 An art and technology centre was opened at Caterham School by Sir Keith Joseph, Secretary of State for Education and Science, on the occasion of the annual Speech Day.

10th 1931 Mr Oscar Wilson Moorson-Roberts of Crowthorne, Berks and Coulsdon, Surrey, died aged 82. According to *The Times* one bequest from his £38,721 estate was of £500 left to Dr Harman Harrigan of Bottesdale in Norfolk "for saving the testator's life on three occasions, and one in particular when he carried him into his own bed and himself slept in a cupboard for several months and refused to make any charge, but eventually accepted a honorarium from his eldest brother."

1944 Air raids disrupted schooling at Kenley Primary School. There were alerts at 9.06 a.m., 10.40 a.m. and 2.20 p.m., the All Clear sounding at 9.30 a.m., 11.02 a.m. and 3.37 p.m. respectively.

11th 1366 An agreement was made "between Thomas de Purlee and brother Thomas de Sallowe master of the house of St Thomas of Acre in London, next to the Conduit. Thomas de Purlee leased all his lands, rents and tenements with woods and pastures in the parishes of Coulsdon and Chaldon, except for his property on the north side of the church of Watendone which he reserves for himself, for 13 years at 6s 8d a year. The master of the house of St Thomas is allowed to take underwood and timber for the repair of the buildings as necessary."

1897 "School closed for holidays early because of Scarlet Fever. The Schoolrooms disinfected." (Kenley National School Log Book)

1944 Kenley Primary School Log Book records more air raids: Alerts at 9.23 a.m., 10.10 a.m., 11.55 a.m., 1.55 p.m. and 3.50 p.m. with the All Clear sounding at 9.48 a.m., 10.30 a.m., 12.38 p.m., 3.40 p.m. and 4.40 p.m.

12th 1938 Near Fairchildes Hubert E. Pounds examined a wren's "nest containing four eggs from which four young ones were eventually reared. This was constructed in a loosely coiled engine-driving belt hanging from a nail inside a rough wooden shed that housed a chaff-cutting machine."

1944 "Miss Little resumed duty today. Miss N.W. Darby is absent from school. She is acting as Party Escort with children evacuated to Leeds." (Kenley Primary School Log Book)

13th 1538 The Building Accounts for Nonsuch Palace for the pay period ending 13th July include reference to the cost of John Maxborne in riding to press-gang workmen from places including Lingfield and Bletchingley. He received 6d a day for 13 days, on top of his wages, for himself and his horse.

1700   John Evelyn recorded a visit to Marden Park: "I went to Marden, which was originally a barren warren bought by Sir Robert Clayton, who built there a pretty house, and made such alteration by planting not only an infinite store of the best fruit, but so changed the natural situation of the hill, valleys and solitary mountains about it, that it rather represented some foreign country."

1888   James Selby drove the *Old Times* coach and horses from London to Brighton and back in under 8 hours, winning a wager of £1,000 for the owners. There were frequent "pit-stops" to change horses—that at the *Windsor Castle* in Purley Oaks took 65 seconds on the outward journey and 50 on the return. His employer gave him the wager money.

14th 1867   Alfred Nobel demonstrated the use of dynamite in a Merstham quarry. To show its safety and stability a case of 10lbs of dynamite was put on a bonfire and burnt, and a similar quantity was thrown from a rock 60 feet high—in neither case was there an explosion. Its power was then successfully demonstrated when it was fired by fuse and detonator. (See 11th August 1869)

1951   A Grand Festival of Britain meeting of Cycle Track Racing and Polo was held at White Knobs Sports Ground, Caterham.

1973   The first flower festival and arts display ever to be held in All Saints Church, Warlingham, took place in the hope of giving pleasure to visitors and raising funds for "The League of Friends of Caterham and Warlingham District Hospitals."

15th 1538   The Building Accounts of Nonsuch Palace for the pay period starting 15th July refer to the purchase of Square Timber from several sources including from Richard Best of Alderstead, Merstham, at 5s and 5s 8d per load (each load was of 50 feet.) He was paid £40 7s 10d in total. Carters from Nutfield, Bletchingley, Merstham, Chipstead, Reigate and Banstead were also employed to transport wagon loads of wood from East Tye at 1s 8d a load.

16th 1685   A Probate Inventory was made "of the goods of Anne Lambert, Widow, of Coulsdon." The total value was £2,273 0s 10d and items included were: "Three Bedds and Bedstedds, three Chests, one Courte Cupboard, three Chayres, three Stooles and one paire of Andirons, Tongs and Fire Shovle and one Truncke" (£16 10s 6d); "Lynnen" (£15 10s); "Wooll" (£44); "Twelve Beere Caskes" (£1 18s); "Seven horses and harness" (£40); "Wagons, Cartes, ploughs and other implements of Husbandry" (£20); "Debts due and owing from severall persons" (£1,745 6s 0d).

1918   A freak hailstorm, only about half a mile wide, swept across Coulsdon, Purley, Kenley and Sanderstead. "At Capt. Alfred Carpenter's house about 30 hailstones came down the chimney to each room and rolled about the floors covered in soot." The hailstones were described by Mr

E.C. Rutherford of Purley as being lemon-shaped. He measured the largest he saw and it had a circumference of 4½ inches.

17th 1885 "Mumps have broken out, & several children with symptoms of them have been sent home. All the Jenners are absent, Diptheria having broken out in their home. The Pupil Teacher was absent on Wednesday, being too ill to attend. Average for the week 71.8." (Kenley National School Log Book)

18th 1576 John Smythe of Chelsham, a labourer, stole a cloak (worth 16d), 4 shirts (1s), a pair of hose (8d), a tunic (5s), a doublet (3s 4d) and a hat (3s) from John Wodden. He was indicted for grand larceny at Croydon Assizes, found guilty but "allowed clergy."

1635 Caterham parish registers contain a Memorandum "that a poore woman whose name was unknowe, but a hatter's wife, was buried."

1831 Henry John Temple, third Viscount Palmerston, was "elected" Member of Parliament for the rotten borough of Bletchingley. (Such boroughs were done away with in 1832.)

19th 1278 The expenses of "Master Peter and his companions" for a day spent at Farleigh were: bread 2½d, ale 8d, salmon 18d, three quarters of herrings 7d, wine 10½d and vinegar 1d.

1775 The cricket match played "in Smytham Bottom, near Croydon, between the Coulsdon Club, Surry, and this County, for £25 a man, was won hollow by the former." *(Sussex Weekly Advertiser)*

20th 1325 A great storm destroyed part of the harvest at Tillingdown.

1683 In Warlingham "Alice Woodden, aged above a 100 yeares, was buryed in woollen only."

1854 Chipstead Fair was suppressed. The following day Tho. Hart described the event in a letter to Sir W. Geo. Hylton Joliffe, Bart, M.P.: "I have the satisfaction to inform you that we succeeded in putting down Chipstead Fair most completely....The Police attended on the spot two days before the Fair and turned away all Vans Carts etc etc as they arrived. There was only one refractory party yesterday and the police disposed of him. I am satisfied a great moral good has been effected and the more so as if we had met with opposition I fear we should have had a great trouble in making out a case 'No Fair'."

21st 1463 At Farleigh manor court it was presented that "All the tenants of Farleigh from time immemorial have pastured their cattle and sheep on the common in Chelsham called Chelsham Heath and now they are prevented from doing this by Thomas Uvedale."

1859 The Caterham Railway Company, after prolonged financial difficulties, was taken over by the South Eastern Railway for £15,200. (It had cost £39,367 to construct.)

1993   Official opening of the M25 Service Station at Clacket Lane, Titsey. Prior to the construction work the Surrey County Archaeology Unit carried out excavations, with some assistance from Bourne Society members, which found evidence of mediaeval pottery kilns and several thousand sherds of pottery on both the northern and southern sides of the motorway.

22nd 1321   The manor of Farleigh paid to the Sheriff of Surrey the sum of 6d as its annual payment of "hundred silver".

1783   In Coulsdon churchyard the burial took place of "William Rivers, aged 25. A most amiable, worthy young man (who) was drowned in the Pound pond at Croydon, & universally lamented by his master & the family & all who knew him."

23rd 1740   In Warlingham "Phillip the son of John Saxby and Mary Quittendon" was baptized. (See 25th March 1739—presumably the same couple?—if so, Mary no longer claims to be his wife.)

1808   The burial took place in Warlingham of "Richard Burt, aged 32 years, killed near Slynes in endeavouring to stop a waggon."

1929   George W. Davies photographed, at the Caterham Council Offices, four objects found in recently dug sewer pipe trenches. One was a 'rapier' found on the north side of Whyteleafe Hill—probably a fairly modern foil, with a blade 28¼" long, square in section and tapering to a short edge, not a point, and with a figure of eight guard. A little south of Wapses Lodge, on the west side of the Godstone Road, were found three iron 'cannon balls', each 3" in diameter.

24th 1805   The opening of the Croydon to Merstham extension (via Purley and Coulsdon) to the Surrey Iron Railway, which had operated from Wandsworth to Croydon since 26th July 1803. The trucks were pulled by mules or horses walking between the tracks, their average speed being around 2½ mph.

25th 1408   At the manor court in Merstham Matilda Dygon was fined 5d for being "a common gossip and disturber of the peace."

1944   A note in the Minute Book of the St Nicholas Youth Fellowship, Godstone, records that "Children evacuated to S. Wales."

26th 1905   "Closed School all day - the Annual Flower Show. Many children exhibit grasses and wild flowers. 18 prizes taken by Kenley Sch. Children. I have assisted the Judges for 21 years but I never remember seeing better bouquet & grasses put up by the Children before....The Children took great zest in searching for Flowers & Grasses this year, they were familiar to most of them, & there was the additional interest of finding something they had not seen or taken notice of before....I think the children who exhibited well earned their holiday." (Kenley National School Log Book)

27th 1949 Mr. J.S.S. Beesley came across the remains, in Oxted, of a rare summer visitor—a Hoopoe. Only five are recorded in the area between 1892 and 1950. This one "had evidently been struck down by a Sparrow-Hawk."

1956 A double retirement at Sanderstead Primary School: Miss Evelyn Lynn, who had been headmistress since 1933, and Mrs Margaret Smith, her senior teacher, who had been at the school since 1936.

28th 1722 This date, with the initials "I.P." form part of the graffiti inside Chaldon stone mines.

1897 St Mary's Church Magazine (Caterham) reported on the Choir Treat: "The weather being favourable, the day at Brighton was very much enjoyed, the members of our party betaking themselves to whatever kind of attraction they most fancied, and assembled together again for the substantial dinner at Booth's Restaurant."

29th 1645 The Revd George Moore, Rector of Chipstead, was summoned to appear before a Parliamentary Committee to answer charges "that he was a common drunkard and swearer." (His living was sequestrated on 16th September 1646.)

30th 1778 At 1 p.m., at the Marlborough Coffee House, there was an auction of "a valuable freehold estate called Cheverells Manor Farm most desirably situate in the Parish of Titsey." It consisted of farmhouse and buildings and 314 acres. It was leased for an annual rent of £141 6s for 46 years from Michaelmas 1774. Included as part of the same lot was a compact leasehold farm called the Holts in Chelsham.

1912 "Large numbers of clouded yellow butterflies have been on the wing this last week. I have not seen them before this for 20 years." (Arthur Beadell's Nature Notes)

31st 1483 At the manor court of Robert Hardyng, lord of the manor of Chelsham Watvyle, Thomas and Richard Kempsall, John Comport and John A. Broke of Farleigh were fined for having wrongly overstocked the lord's common with their animals—more than their "fair share."

AUGUST

1st 1893 The Warlingham & District Cottage Garden Society held its summer show. Competition categories included window plant, specimen plant, bouquet of cut flowers, red currants, 1 plate, potatoes round and potatoes kidney, peas, 12 pods, beetroot, best bird fowls, best rabbit, pigs—3 to 6 months old only....and, under Home Industry: Boy's suit made from old garments, honey in comb, article of fancy work, knitted stockings or socks (girls under 15), men's trousers. "Most of the prizes were donated by the gentry who lived on the larger estates in the district."

Plate XV

The Caterham Centenarian special train passing through Whyteleafe South

— see 6th August 1956

Plate XVI

Chelsham church and churchyard

— see 20th August 1604

Plate XVII

The new bells at St Nicholas' Church, Godstone were dedicated
on 16th September 1915

Plate XVIII

The Woldingham section of the Outer London Defences
under construction

— see 20th September 1915

Plate XIX

R.C.A.F. Dakota crashed in a Purley garden

— see 19th October 1945

Reproduced by kind permission of the Croydon Advertiser Group Limited

Plate XX

Ike the soldier monkey at Gardner's Pleasure Resort at Riddlesdown

Plate XXI (inset) — Ike's cast-iron 'tombstone'

— see 1st November 1913

Plate XXII

The house at Marden Park

— see 9th November 1879

Plate XXIII

The Warlingham Almshouses (established on 18th November
1675) are on the left-hand side of the picture

Plates XXIV and XXIVb (detail)

The 'gibbet post' built into a Purley Oaks barn

— see 21st November 1955 and 30th December 1955

Reproduced by kind permission of Croydon Libraries, Museum & Arts

Plate XXV

Prince Arthur at the opening of the Boys' Club in Chipstead Valley Road

— see 25th November 1935

Reproduced by kind permission of Croydon Libraries, Museum & Arts

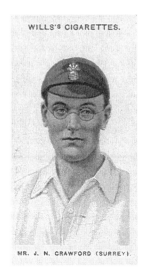

WILLS'S CIGARETTES.
MR. J. N. CRAWFORD (SURREY).

Plate XXVI

Cigarette card no. 35 in Wills' Cricketers series

— see 1st December 1886

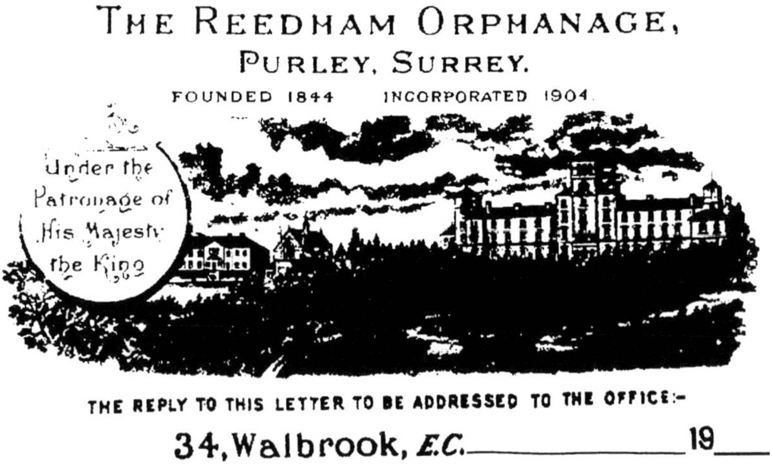

THE REEDHAM ORPHANAGE,
PURLEY, SURREY.
FOUNDED 1844 INCORPORATED 1904.
Under the Patronage of His Majesty the King
THE REPLY TO THIS LETTER TO BE ADDRESSED TO THE OFFICE:-
34, Walbrook, E.C. 19

Plate XXVII

Letterhead of The Reedham Orphanage

— see 16th December 1880

Reproduced by kind permission of Croydon Libraries, Museum & Arts

Plate XXVIII

Work on the Woldingham section of the Outer London Defences

— see 16th December 1917

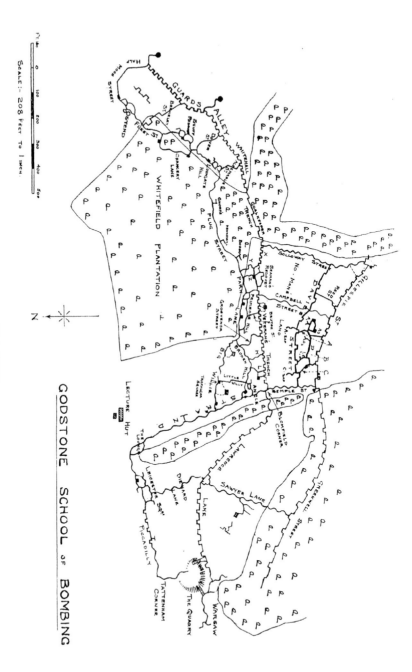

Plate XXIX

The Godstone School of Bombing in Marden Park
— see 19th December 1915

2nd   1871   A match was played on the Cricket Ground in Upper Caterham between Caterham and Croydon Bohemians. The Caterham team won the game, scoring 64 and 77 against the Bohemians 53 and 32.

1901   Two internationally celebrated golfers, James Braid and Harry Vardon, made an appearance at Warlingham Golf Club.

3rd   1905   "The school closed this afternoon for summer holidays Aug 3 - Sept 4. During the warm weather the temperature of the Schoolrooms has often gone up to 82 - 84 degrees. Fortunately our children are clean, particularly the girls, otherwise it would be very unpleasant at such times. The 1st Std & Upper Class of Infants are taken outside for convenient lessons alternately, & this arrangement has relieved the Infants Room. We are, however, very glad to close for a respite...." (Kenley National School Log Book)

1912   "English partridges nest with 8 eggs on Riddlesdown. There were hundreds of people walking all round where the partridge was sitting undisturbed." (Arthur Beadell's Nature Notes)

4th   1661   Sanderstead parish collected "7s 3d for the Towne of Milton Abbas in Dorsetshire; Delivered to Edmund Coale, Sep. 18 1662."

1779   Warlingham parish collected "the sum of Twelve shillings and sixpence By Virtue of his Majesty's Letter of Recommendation to be paid to the Treasurer of the Society for the Propagation of the Gospel in Foreign Parts, towards the relief and for the continuance of the said Society."

1856   The official opening of the Caterham Railway (from Purley Station—then called Caterham Junction—to Caterham). A special train left London Bridge at 12.15 p.m. and arrived at about 1 p.m. It was met by a large crowd, headed by one of its local Directors, Alfred Smith, farmer, of Tupwood. He weighed 20 stone and was described in one report as "a practical illustration of the proverb 'laugh and grow fat'."

1926   Mr Weston of Caterham on the Hill, writing to his landlord concerning the possession of land on the corner of Chaldon Road and Heath Road, was prepared to give up the land on condition that he had "access to the Haystack for the purpose of taking it away during the next 6 months."

5th   1659   The Council of State ordered Major Lewis Audeley of Sanderstead (see 16th August 1650) to recruit more men for his Troop of Horse, to replace those he had lost. (Calendar of State Papers)

1856   The Caterham Railway line opened to the public, for goods and passengers. To attract more custom annual season tickets were offered for travel to and from London—to those building houses on the Company's property—at a fare of £7 First Class and £5 Second Class.

6th   1956   At 10.45 a.m. *The Caterham Centenarian* special steam train, hauled by *Morden*, a former London, Brighton & South Coast Railway "Terrier" engine built in June 1878, and painted in the original livery, departed from platform 6 at Purley Station for Caterham, where it was open to public inspection until 2.20 p.m. *(Plate XV)*

1981   An eight mile high cumulo-nimbus thundercloud passed over East Surrey, making midday as dark as midnight. The thunderstorm which followed was one of the worst in living memory.

7th   1944   In an outbuilding at Broom Lodge in Chelsham Hubert E. Pounds "examined an unusual type of nest which had been constructed by a pair of Swallows for their second brood. This was not placed, as is customary, upon a horizontal beam or other similar projection affording support, but was attached to a wooden partition dividing the interior of the building, and viewed from below bore resemblance to a nest of the House-Martin."

1947   Mr Felix, Clerk of Coulsdon and Purley U.D.C., wrote to the Chief Librarian seeking assistance in replying to a letter from a resident of Tollers Lane, Old Coulsdon, "who is desirous of grazing a goat on Bradmore Green" and who understood that "it is an old law that the goat is 'the poor Man's cow' and can be grazed on common land."

8th   1899   The "Mothers' Meeting of St Mary's Church Caterham gathered at Sunnyside for their garden party and presented their hostess Miss Guimaraens with a charming case of cut-glass scent bottles." (Church Magazine)

1947   The Chief Librarian replied to yesterday's letter, giving details of the Rights of Common in Coulsdon Manor, saying that "it would seem that a present day owner or occupier of a parcel must have at least one acre to be entitled to graze one beast upon the waste." The resident probably therefore had no right of Common pasture, but he pointed out that the Council, as Lord of the Manor, could grant her a licence to graze her goat on Bradmore Green.

1983   Purley fountain was formally reopened by the Mayor of Croydon, Mrs Margaret Campbell, in its new location in the grounds of the Library.

9th   1380   "Sir Reynold de Cobham of Starborough, lord of the manor of Oxted, married Eleanor, former wife of Sir John Arundell, both knowing they were in the third degree of consanguinity. In this unlawful marriage they had three children. (See 26th September 1384) (Calendar of Inquisitions)

1919   The Coulsdon Cinema was showing "Wm S. Hart in another masterpiece on Sea and Land - *Shark Monroe.*" Also the "Sensational Serial *The Circus King* " with "Mutt and Jeff Cartoons, Paramount World Travels, Arbuckle and Sennett Comedies, and Gaumont Graphics."

10th   1892   "Splendid day, very warm. Men took 4 waggons of flints and 2 carts to Kenley Hotel. The mothers meeting excursion to Eastbourne - Emma & Joe & Maggie went with mother. Had a splendid day." (Beech Farm Diaries)

1943 "Marden Park - Work is proceeding on a 30 yd range for small arms and a miniature Range for Arty practice. It is hoped these will be in use as soon as possible." (War Diary 2nd Medium Regiment R.C.A.)

11th 1615 "I rode to Lingfield to a sessions for a Ryott between Lady Borough's servants and George Howden." (Lady Catherine Borough, a widow, lived at Starborough Castle. She died in 1622.) (Bostock Fuller J.P.)

1869 An Act of Parliament prohibited the manufacture, import, sale and transportation of explosives containing nitroglycerine within Great Britain, illustrating the failure of Alfred Nobel to convince the Government of the safety of dynamite by his demonstration in a Merstham quarry. (See 14th July 1867)

1974 The Bourne Society held an open afternoon at their archaeological excavations at Lagham Manor in South Godstone. More than 200 people attended. For some reason the *Surrey Mirror* had advertised it as "Nature Show open Sunday."

12th 1538 The Building Accounts of Nonsuch Palace for the pay period starting today include reference to the payment of 8d a day for 6 days to John Life, for himself and his horse, in riding to East Tye, Godstone, Burstow Wood and Rutherwick (in Long Ditton) to select timber for the Palace.

13th 1771 *The Sussex Weekly Advertiser* reported that at the cricket match played on 13th and 14th August at Henfield the home team were defeated by Coulsdon Cricket Club "by 4 or 5 wickets." They had won the first match at Smitham Bottom by five wickets.

1946 "Boating at Lines. We had the misfortune to break a number of oars, but Mrs Lines said they could easily be mended. A committee meeting was held in the middle of Lines Pond attended by three members. Two weeks programmes were arranged." (Minute Book of St Nicholas Youth Fellowship, Godstone)

14th 1868 "It was resolved that the Vestry having been convinced of the dangerous state of the ceiling of the Parish Church, the Churchwardens be requested to take such steps as they may find necessary to remedy the defects." (Caterham Churchwardens' Accounts)

1953 K.M. Newbury and Dr S.J. Madge visited a solicitor's office in Essex to see whether or not the collection of manorial records there related to the Coulsdon and Purley Urban District. The only relevant documents were an incomplete set of Sanderstead manorial rolls covering the period 1511 to 1678. They advised the Council that £40 should be the maximum offer made to purchase them.

15th 1887 Her Majesty's Inspector reported on Kenley National School: "Mixed School - The School has passed a highly satisfactory Examination in all the Subjects both Elementary and Special. The Elementary work throughout is of the best. Both Grammar and Geography are answered fully and with great intelligence. Recitation is considerably above the average. Needlework is good. Singing is to be commended. The order is excellent. Infants Class - The Infants do their work throughout very nicely and are much above the average in regard to intelligence and familiarity with things about them. Needlework is very fairly good, except that there is no Needle Drill. Singing is good. For Marching the space is too confined. Better provision would be made for suitable Occupations if Kindergarten were taught."

1940 A.R.P. wardens reported "Enemy plane down at Redhill Aerodrome. Two enemy parachutists apprehended by Military between Bletchingley and Nutfield."

16th 1650 In the 18th century a document was found in Purley Place House, as it was then called (formerly known as West Purley and later as Purley Bury House), signed by John Bradshaw (President of the High Court of Justice at the trial of Charles I) and dated today, appointing Major Lewis Audeley, who lived there, "to be Captaine of a Troup of Horse of such well affected persons as takeing the Engagement shall be Listed under you in the County of Surrey."

17th 1895 A cricket match was played in the grounds of Ledgers Park between Mr R.H.A. Daniell's Eleven and Chelsham. The Chelsham and Warlingham Parish Magazine reported that "This proved to be a very exciting as well as a most pleasant game, Mr Daniell's side winning in the first innings by 2 runs. Scores: The Ledgers (Mr R. Daniell's Eleven) 80, Chelsham 78."

1915 "A thunderstorm occurred in the afternoon of the 17th when, in less than ten minutes, the lawn had become a raging torrent, which raced through the gate into the road, where the water stretched from side to side. In less than 40 minutes nearly an inch-and-a-half had fallen." (Description by Mrs Harris at *The Larches* in the Chelsham and Warlingham Parish Magazine)

18th 1940 There was a big lunch time air raid on Kenley Aerodrome. A Dornier 17 crashed into a house in Golf Road, Kenley, killing the crew of five. Three Croydon Hurricanes crashed—at Chelsham, Tatsfield and Banstead.

1940 The *Sun Bathing Review* reported the same raid as viewed from the Nu-Radient Health Club in Warlingham: "while forty or fifty members were sipping their cups, seated about the club terrace, a group of Nazi planes appeared at the other side of the valley and began dropping bombs. But none of the members, according to my correspondent, raced for shelter. They continued sipping their tea, knowing that the proper department would deal with the visitors and, presently, an R.A.F squadron appeared, annoyed doubtless at being disturbed at such an hour, and blasted the Germans into fragments in an unhurried but highly efficient manner."

1943　"Marden Park - Fine Harvest weather. A number of men and personnel are engaged at harvesting under the Agricultural Assistance Scheme." (War Diary 2nd Medium Regiment R.C.A.)

19th　1889　Riddlesdown School (for Infants and older) moved into new premises—the Juniors were separated and became Purley National Mixed School and the Infants became Purley National Infants School under Miss Elizabeth A. Bishop.

1919　"A Film Masterpiece - *Dormant Power* " was showing at The Coulsdon Cinema, which was under the management of Mr and Mrs Wallis Barrington. The programme also contained "the Thrilling Serial *Judex*." Their advertisement said "Forget Weather Worries in Coulsdon's Cool Cinema." Admission was 1/3d, 1/- and 8d for adults and 10d, 8d, and 5d for children accompanied by adults.

20th　1604　In his will, Thomas Leigh, yeoman, of Fairchilds in Chelsham, requested that he be buried "by his ancestors" at the east end of the chancel in Chelsham churchyard. As well as numerous bequests to his family, including £4 to each of his many grandchildren (to the boys at 21 and the girls at 18 or on marriage, if earlier), he left 10 shillings "To the poor man's boy in Chelsham." *(Plate XVI)*

1870　*The Croydon Advertiser,* quoting a London paper, contained a description of "the Tillingdown rifle-ground, where sharp practice is indulged in on certain days of the week by gentlemen who go down from London and Croydon. It is a capital ground and the shooters have it all to themselves without fear of molestation or breaking in upon the quiet of anybody."

1892　"Lovely warm day. Dulake took 11½ qtrs of wheat to Brown's & brought back flour, bran etc....Dulake came home drunk & quarrelsome & broke our windows." (Beech Farm Diaries)

21st　1858　Caterham—The Fair: "Owing to the disturbances of late years at this fair the leading inhabitants intend to apply for its suppression. The fair is held in the street and the result is that in the evening the village is filled with drunken men and the usual attendants at places of that description, thereby causing a great nuisance to the respectable portion of the inhabitants. The fines inflicted by the magistrates do not deter them from assaulting the police year after year. The only remedy, therefore, is the entire suppression of the fair, which will be a real benefit to the village." *(Sussex Agricultural Express)*

1943　"Marden Park - Harvesting in full progress with about 100 men and 20-25 vehicles employed." (War Diary 2nd Medium Regiment R.C.A.)

22nd 1896 Warlingham Cricket Club played at home against Sydenham, losing by 18 runs—Sydenham 53, Warlingham 35. Most of the Warlingham runs were obtained by T. Church (18) and S. Dean (8).

1982 30 members of the Bourne Society went on 'an exploration' of Alderstead Heath, with visits to Cold Blow (the aptly named former gamekeeper's cottage), Alderstead Farm (with its huge open fireplace and its wig pegs) and the Victorian fort.

23rd 1947 Hubert E. Pounds observed an Ortolan Bunting "by the almost dried-up dew-pond on the summit of Nore Hill, near Chelsham. The bird maintained a crouching posture all the time I watched it, with its back partly towards me, so that I was unable to see its breast, under-parts or legs, though several times it turned its head furtively in my direction....Encircling the eye, which was black, was a most conspicuous yellow ring or 'spectacle', and extending downward from the back a pronounced, rather broad, yellowish streak."

24th 1653 A heading in the marriage section of Sanderstead parish register says: "The persons hereafter named were married by Lewes Audeley, Esqr, one of the Justices of the Peace in this County att his house in Saunderstead according to a late Act of Parlyament entituled an Act touching Marriages & the Registring thereof &c. Dated 24th Aug 1653." (The marriages listed are from 28th January 1653 to 3rd June 1658.)

1753 "A Lad about 18 or 19 years of age" who had been employed as a Whipper-in to the hounds of Sir Kenrick Clayton at Marden was suspected of stealing a horse and its equipment today. A reward was offered for his capture and conviction. The suspect was described as "Middle sized of a pale Complection and a mole upon his Jawbone on the side of his Chin with a long Hair upon the mole." When he went away he was wearing "a Green plush Coat, an orange colloured cloth Wainscott Double Breasted with white Mettall Buttons, a pair of new Buckskin Breeches, new Boots single turned down, a Black velvet Capp with a Cutt in the Front." He was seen subsequently in Croydon, riding the stolen horse, and wearing "a Brown Fustian Frock." (See 15th May 1754)

25th 1934 The grand opening of the swimming pool at the Nu-Radient Health Club in Warlingham (later The White House Club). There had been a prolonged dry spell and water had to be brought in a "fleet of United Dairies milk tankers. These were cleaned out and filled with water from an artesian well in the Purley area and by a succession of trips the pool was thus one quarter filled." The Club's official history records that "Since the press and a few other non-members were present, costumes were worn....Once the visitors had departed, off came the costumes and the members reverted to normal."

1943 "Harvest operations are nearly complete and farmers are well pleased with the work of the men." (War Diary 2nd Medium Regiment R.C.A.)

26th 1837 Patrick Carrol, a sojourner from Limerick, age 35, was buried by order of the coroner, having been "killed by a blow."

1873 A meeting was held at the Metropolitan District Asylum (later called St Lawrence's Hospital) to "consider the advisability of forming a new Cricket Club for Caterham."

27th 1940 *The Weekly Press and County Post* reported that "there was great excitement at 2.30 on the Tuesday morning when a Heinkel 3 bomber returning from London was hit by gunfire and eventually crashed on the edge of Queen's Park, Caterham Hill. Unfortunately it mostly fell on a villa, which was destroyed by the fire that followed the impact. Happily the occupants escaped severe injury....The five Germans who formed the crew baled out, and they were rounded up by A.R.P. wardens, police, and Home Guard, and taken to the local police station."

28th 1532 Robert Grame of Burstow, a collier (i.e. a charcoal burner) was murdered near Crowhurst in Tandridge Hundred, "and his purse lay upon him open and never a penny in it." The local Justice of the Peace, Sir John Gaynesford, on whose land the crime was committed, has left a detailed report of his attempt to bring the perpetrators to justice. This report, made to Thomas Cromwell, makes it one of the best documented cases of its type and time. The alleged murderers were John Comport the younger, of Godstone, a husbandman, and John Benson his servant. John Comport supplemented his income by using his own wagon to haul goods for others, including Robert Grame. Despite the detailed record the final outcome is not known.

29th 1742 Bletchingley churchwardens paid out one shilling cash "for nailing a Foxes Head at the Church Gate" and another shilling to a "Traveller with a Pass."

1930 The *Coulsdon and Purley Weekly Record* reported on the funeral of Mr William Webb in Coulsdon. He was the planner behind the "Garden First Development" exemplified by the Woodcote Estate. He was also the instigator of the Promenade de Verdun as a memorial to French soldiers killed in the Great War.

30th 1749 Croydon parish register records that "James Cooper, a highwayman, was executed on a gibbet in Smitham Bottom, and there hanged in chains for the murdering and robbing of Robert Saxby near Crome Hurst."

1764 The burial took place in Coulsdon of Robert Thornton, "a poor man supported by this parish....& thirty years before he died he left off coming to Church upon the account of some disgust he took at the Rector of those times."

1803   Sarah Roffey, wife of Henry "a private militia man serving in the militia", had moved from their home parish of Chaldon to Horley. The local J.P. ordered payment of "£2, being four shillings a week from 17/6 to 26/8 (& then 4/- weekly thereafter) for the support & maintenance of Sarah & her child Maria, aged about 2 months" by Horley's Guardians of the Poor. They were to recover the money from Chaldon's Overseers.

1940   Chelsham A.R.P. Wardens' Post reported "1 Enemy fighter down at Ficklesholes Farm, Chelsham. No damage."

31st   1782   Richard, the son of James and Sarah Lord, was baptised at the *Rose and Crown.*

1897   "The belated examination for prizes given by Mrs Daniell was held at the Chelsham and Farleigh School....The prizes for 'progress in work' and 'Good Conduct' were designed to perpetuate the memory of this notable year and consisted of framed pictures of our Queen and 'Jubilee Mugs'. Books were the reward for attendance." (See 6th Sept 1897) (Warlingham and Chelsham Parish Magazine)

1940   *The Weekly Press and County Post* reported that an enemy aeroplane "was brought down at Tillingdown, and the German who baled out was found at Oxted."

SEPTEMBER

1st   1612   Farleigh manor "court declares that Edmund Eyres gentleman, has not demolished part of the cottage that he had built on the lord's waste in a place called Farleigh Green. He is fined £5."

1891   "School re-opened this morning - the Managers having accepted the Fee Grant in lieu of School Pence, the School is in consequence quite free to the children." (Kenley National School Log Book)

1939   Kenley Church of England School for Junior and Mixed Infants closed "as they had no air raid shelters." The children re-assembled at Kenley Council School in New Barn Lane.

2nd   1716   Sanderstead parish collected 7s 1d for a brief for St Mary's in Colchester.

1739   Caterham parish collected 9s 9d for a brief for Standon in Herefordshire which had suffered from a hail storm.

3rd   1740   Bletchingley churchwardens paid sixpence to a "great Belly'd Woman" and a shilling to a "woman att Town."

1897   During the night "Warlingham Church was broken into by thieves. An attempt was first made to force the small priest's door in the Chancel, the Vestry scraper being torn up for the purpose. This attempt proving ineffectual, an entrance was made by breaking one of the windows in the South Aisle. The Vestry was ransacked, but there was fortunately nothing of value to be found." (Warlingham and Chelsham Parish Magazine)

4th 1940 "21.32: F Division report large bright light at Woldingham Ridge extending towards Titsey. 21.52: E Division report bright flares falling in direction of Chaldon. 22.00: D Division report descent of parachute flares. 22.04: Police report 10 parachutists landing in Worms Heath, Woldingham and that they will be attending. 22.20: Police asked for further information re parachutists, & they replied that Officers were investigating & would let us know. 23.45: Police reports no parachutists found." (Brief extracts from a very busy A.R.P. day recorded in the Red to White Log Book of the Caterham and Warlingham Urban District Report and Control Centre, which was housed under the Soper Hall in Caterham)

5th 1658 Sanderstead parish made a collection for the inhabitants of Wapping, in Middlesex, who had been "distressed by blast of gunpowder." They raised "Sixteen shillings an a pennie."

        1873 A Coulsdon Vestry Minute records that the new length of highway (some 2,400 feet long and 30 feet wide) made at the expense of Joseph Tucker of Portnalls Farm, across Picket Field and Velvet Field, was authorised by the Vestry and was to be dedicated to the public.

6th 1888 "A wedding in the afternoon; Miss Websters, the choir boys being required to attend, and so many other children wishing to do the same, the school was not opened in the afternoon." (Kenley National School Log Book)

        1897 (See 31st August 1897) The Chelsham & Farleigh School prizes were presented "at 'Ledgers' on the occasion of the summer school treat. As the treat had been pushed back so late in the year by the failure of the examination to hold itself sooner, and as the weather just then was so unpleasant, there seemed small hope of a successful out-door treat. Happily the event falsified the gloomy anticipations." (Warlingham and Chelsham Parish Magazine)

        1940 The first bomb—an incendiary—to fall on Chipstead in the Second World War fell in Coulsdon Lane.

7th 1948 "Team games with large ball, which went through window first throw. 'Phoned Mr Kent & he repaired it next morning 17/s." (Minute Book of St Nicholas Youth Fellowship, Godstone)

        1992 The Bourne Society's Natural History Group took a walk around "Godstone under threat". The "threat" is from proposed housing development on Hilly Field, which is probably the only unimproved meadow on sandstone remaining in the area, from the infilling of the reservoirs to create an east-west by-pass and from more possible development around the site of the former Ivy Mill lake.

8th 1755 In Merstham "James son of William and Mary Hart, Travellers from Ramsgate in the Isle of Thanet Kent was born in the Parsonage Stable."

1895 "The Cottage Hospital, now under the capable management of the new Matron (Miss Slark) benefited by the offertory at the Church on Sept. 8th to the amount of £18 4s 5d." (St John's Church Magazine, Caterham Valley)

9th 1912 "This morning marks a new era in the history of the education of Warlingham. Teachers and scholars have met after the midsummer holidays for the first time in the new, beautiful and finely equipped school." (Log Book of Farleigh County First School- quoted in the 1982 70th Anniversary Evening Programme.)

1919 "Fifteen girls taken out by Miss Harrison to pick Blackberries. 18lbs were obtained but as this was under the minimum amount to be sent to a jam factory (20lbs) Miss Harrison sold them to a local fruiterer at 3d per lb since the fruit would not keep until more was obtained." (as previous item)

10th 1646 A lease was agreed between "Sir Francis Carew of Beddington and Thomas Rowett of Coulsdon for the property called Le Roake together with all his warren and game of coneys and all the wood sheep walks and common rights belonging to it in the Parishes of Coulsdon and Warlingham for 21 years. (Memorandum: it is agreed that Thomas Rowett will cherish and maintain the game of coneys upon the land called Le Roake.)"

1715 Warlingham parish "Collected on the Cowkeeper's brief" the sum of 10s.2d.

11th 1891 "School closed today, it being the day for the Sunday School treat. The children have gone to Seaford." (Kenley National School Log Book)

1940 "A shower of incendiaries fell over the Markfield and Markville estate on the Godstone-road at Caterham on the night of September 11th at ten o'clock, but luckily not one struck a housetop, and A.R.P wardens soon extinguished those on the ground. The plane that dropped them passed on and discharged three H.E. bombs over the Queen's Park and other parts of the hill. There was considerable damage, and two fatal casualties were amongst those recorded." *(Weekly Press and County Post)*

12th 1902 "For some weeks past great hinderance to school work has resulted from the running of extra and heavier trains upon the Brighton line. The noise is so great.....that I am not able to make myself heard.....discipline consequently suffers." (Log Book of Maple Road Junior (Mixed) School, Whyteleafe)

1940 St. Margaret's Church in Chipstead was damaged by a parachute landmine.

13th 1797 "John Broad, who was a month's man to John Fuller at the Court, & was drown'd in the pond in the yard" was buried in Coulsdon.

1940 The Caterham Report Centre recorded that "In Holt Wood, near Croydon Mental Hospital, Chelsham" four High Explosive bombs were dropped at 13.20, but did no damage.

1940 Warden Post 12 reported an incident in Chelsham: "1 UXB in field adjoining Ledgers Park 22.30 hrs. No damage. UXB reported to Surrey Control."

14th 1755 James Hart (see 8th September 1755) was baptized in Merstham.

1878 In the Regimental Orders of the Second Surrey Rifles the Commanding Officer notified the corps, with regret, of the decease of their Honorary Colonel, Lieutenant-Colonel A.D. Wigsell. "Officers will wear mourning, when in uniform, for two months."

1902 In Warlingham, "Pretoria Annie, daughter of Charles and Fanny Jane Davis" was baptised, so named after the Treaty of Pretoria which ended the Boer War earlier the same year. (It could have been worse: a Music Hall song recounted the naming of the Blobbs child—

> "The baby's name is Kitchener Carrington
> Methuen Kekewich White
> Cronje Plumer Powell Majuba
> Gatacre Warren Colenso Kruger
> Capetown Mafeking French
> Kimberley Ladysmith Bobs
> Union Jack Fighting Mac
> Lyddite Pretoria BLOBBS.")

1940 At 12.30 hours—"Capt. Swan and Lieut. Foster take strong advance party to Caterham placing them in houses on each end of Matlock Road to hold same against all comers, particularly R.A.F. billeting officer who claimed priority. Party i/c L/Sgt. Samson." (War Diary 3rd Canadian Infantry Anti-Tank Company)

15th 1912 "Primroses in flower. Large flock of linnets on stubbles." (Arthur Beadell's Nature Notes)

1940 "As there is not enough room in the vicinity for the Company, we had to hunt up entire new quarters. This we found over between the Guards Barracks and the Airport. Many bombs had been dropped around here and the people had moved away, leaving plenty of vacant houses for us." (War Diary 4th Field Company R.C.E.)

16th 1705 In Tatsfield "John, an exposed Child taken up at More-House, was Baptized." (See 26th Nov 1706)

1892 "Went to Tandridge Park Cattle Show, saw Mr Gower's son thrown from his horse and hurt." (Beech Farm Diaries)

1915   Dedication by the Lord Bishop of the Diocese of the new bells (see 10th June 1914) and church clock at St Nicholas Church, Godstone. The clock, with two 4ft 6ins diameter dials, was paid for out of a £120 legacy from J.D. Charlton Esq. The work was carried out by Gillett and Johnson of Croydon. *(Plate XVII)*

17th 1812   The churchwardens of Chaldon paid 3s 6d to Richard Wheadon, Apparitor, "To Prayers for the repeated Successes obtained over the French Army in Portugal and Spain, and also amended Prayer."

1878   "The annual Merstham pleasure fair" was held today and "was the scene of a miscellaneous collection of shows, stalls and general itinerates, with the filling up of crowds and groups of idlers and lookers-on. It is a great day or night for the Mersthamites, and they make the most of it, the licensed houses being especially well patronised." *(Croydon Advertiser)*

18th 1940   "1400 hrs - Unit moves to Caterham, the billeting area for winter. Caterham is a little town, in a valley, half a mile wide and some ten miles long. The town itself is in the valley and most residential houses are on the hills. Troops are comfortably placed in the houses. Our headquarters are in a beautiful residence called EDGEMOUNT." (War Diary Royal 22e Regiment, Canadian Active Service Force)

19th 1866   A grave-board "In Memory of W.M. Rogers born at Godstone, Surrey, England" who died on this day stands in the cemetery of the gold-rush town of Barkerville in British Columbia.

1940   "Fine day. Large scale air battle takes place over Bletchingley and Redhill in full view of us" (in Caterham). (War Diary 3rd Canadian Infantry Anti-Tank Company)

20th 1915   The 1st Volunteer Battalion The Queens was allotted by the London District Command the construction of a portion of the Outer London Defences at Willey Farm, Caterham and Aldercombe. (See 16th Dec 1917) *(Plate XVIII)*

1992   Members of the Bourne Society went on a coach outing to look at the historical aspects of the bird and animal houses at London Zoo (as well as at their inhabitants) and then to the Chelsea Physic Garden to study the history of herbs and other plant species.

21st 1888   "Commenced singing by note this week - I was much surprised and pleased with the results, the children picking up the notes readily & singing the intervals with remarkable accuracy." (Kenley National School Log Book)

1940   "Caterham - a landing ground is very close to our company billets, and it is a great sight to see 'Spitfires' and 'Hurricanes' roar over our heads and rush at the enemy." (War Diary Royal 22e Regiment C.A.S.F.)

22nd 1473 A Rental of this date records that Robert Harding, a London goldsmith, rented lands and tenements at Fickleshole, that had previously belonged to Sir Thomas Cook, for an annual rent of 23s 7d and one red rose.

1975 As part of the celebration of 300 years of the Warlingham Almshouses, a coffee morning was held at the vicarage with a fashion display by "The House of Fashion."

23rd 1723 Robert Davis paid a visit to a recently abandoned firestone quarry at Chaldon and inscribed his name and the date on a wall deep inside the underground workings.

1940 "The 1st Canadian Divisional Signals moved into winter quarters" in Bletchingley "and at once began to make themselves agreeable to the people." (*The Half-Million* by C.P.Stacey and Barbara M. Wilson) (See 26th Sept 1940)

24th 1904 "Purrs from Purley by Persian" *(Croydon Advertiser)* reported "Coming up the lane" (Foxley Lane) "master saw a portentous-looking machine in one of the front gardens, and was told that it was the new patent vacuum cleaner, of which Mr C. Booth, at Amberley, higher up the lane, is understood to be the inventor. This wonderful machine extracts every particle of dust from a room and renders such old fashioned methods as carpet beating, chair and sofa banging, and other crude expedients things of the past."

1916 Zeppelin L31 dropped four 128lbs high explosive bombs on the Downscourt Road/Hall Way area of Purley.

25th 1939 "Five Shelters provided by authorities now completed. 40 chn. attended for games." (Kenley Primary School Log Book)

1978 *The Daily Telegraph* published an obituary to Admiral Sir Charles Woodhouse who had died, aged 85, two days previously. The Admiral, of Westhall Road, Warlingham, had commanded the cruiser *Ajax* which, with the *Exeter* and *Achilles*, defeated the German pocket battleship *Graf Spee* in the battle of the River Plate in December 1939.

26th 1384 On Monday September 26th 1384 Sir Reynold de Cobham of Starborough, lord of the manor of Oxted, and his wife Eleanor (see 9th August 1380) "were divorced & separated from the Monday until the following Thursday and were then remarried with apostolic authority and dispensation." (Calendar of Inquisitions)

1940 The 1st Canadian Divisional Signals helped in the moving of furniture out of the bomb damaged area of Bletchingley. Their assistance earned a letter of thanks from the local Women's Voluntary Service.

27th 1940 "0.25 hours - Lone plane drops two bombs, one in front garden of 11 Matlock Road and second demolishes garage of 12 Matlock Road," (Caterham) "considerable damage is done to neighbouring bungalows but there are no casualties. Sentries are posted at each end of street to insure against casualties from live electric wires lying in roadway." (War Diary 3rd Canadian Infantry Anti-Tank Company)

1940 "Caterham 10.00 - The fiercest air battle yet seen by any one of us is witnessed over our heads: enemy fighter escort and bombers were engaged by our squadrons of fighters. Fighter escort was broken and the bombers were shot down. In all seven fighters and twelve bombers of the enemy were destroyed. Three 'Spitfires' were seen to come down." (War Diary Royal 22e Regiment C.A.S.F.)

28th 1759 The Reverend Mr Thomas Herring of Coulsdon "let all the Glebe and Tithes to Edward Roffey, Thomas Winch, Bray Lucas, Henry Rowed & Richard Roffey, reserving to himself the House free from all Taxes (except the Window Tax), the Fold-Yard, the running of Hogs, Pigs & Fowls in the Fold-Yard, the Hogsties, Duck-House, Hen-House, the New Stable in the Fold-Yard & the Stable in the Dial-Plat, from Michaelmas day then next ensuing for three years during his Incumbencey for the Yearly rent of 200£ at half-yearly payments, Lady Day and Michaelmas the first payment to be made at Lady day the next ensuing, free from all Taxes."

1815 Chaldon churchwardens paid two shillings and sixpence "To Apparitors fee - Thanksgiving Prayer for Victory obtained at Waterloo."

1940 "Several of the ladies of Woldingham have volunteered to furnish a large room in the Bn H.Q. house, Southdean, for the officers' mess and have done a very creditable job, so that we now have some place to spend an hour or two." (War Diary West Nova Scotia Regiment)

29th 1170 Michaelmas—The Sheriff of Surrey rendered "an account for 40s from the hundred of Tandridge for one murder. 20s paid into the treasury and 20s owing." (The remainder was paid in instalments, finishing at Michaelmas 1178) (Pipe Rolls)

1326 The accounts for Bletchingley manor dated today include some wage details: 4d for one man for laying shingles on the grange for a day; 2s 3d for 2 men hired for 18 days to separate the chaff from the wheat, to clean the seed, at three farthings per day; 4d for trimming one oak tree blown down by the wind and making planks from it and sawing them; 4d for one thatcher hired to thatch the mill called Daberonnesmelle for 1 day for himself and his workman.

1350 The wages of a thatcher and his assistant at Woldingham were increased to 6d a day because of the Black Death causing a labour shortage.

1430 The windmill at Bletchingley was dismantled at a cost of 6s 2d, which included the provision of bread and ale for 12 men.

1870 The Caterham Metropolitan Asylum—later St Lawrence's Hospital—was opened "for the relief & reception of poor persons who were mentally handicapped or mentally ill....The patients came to Caterham from overcrowded London Workhouses and, in fact, the hospital itself was then legally classed as a workhouse."

1904   Directors of the Caterham and District Gas Company decided to buy a thousand tickets of admission to the Gas Exhibition at Earl's Court that autumn and distribute them amongst their customers. They also granted three weeks' leave of absence "to the secretary so that he could visit a gasworks at Bastia, in Corsica."

30th   1544   Thomas Hurlock the baker was fined five shillings at Warlingham manor court, for selling bread made with adulterated flour and for overcharging.

1651   Warlingham manor court fined John Batt fourpence for building a cottage on Warlingham heath without permission.

1940   "Woldingham - Passes to Caterham were cancelled when it was learned that the boys were arranging a meeting with the Guards, whose Depot is at Caterham. This seems to be a recurrence of the Camberley affair, after which it was thought that 'the hatchet had been buried.' It is hoped that with Provost Serjeant Lupton on the look-out another battle with the Guards may be averted." (War Diary West Nova Scotia Regiment)

OCTOBER

1st   1283   At Acton Burnell Edward I gave a "Grant to Gilbert de Clare, earl of Gloucester & Hertford, of a yearly fair at his manor of Blescingeleye, Surrey, on the vigil, the feast and the morrow of All Saints." (Calendar of Charter Rolls)

1765   At Chelsham manor court it was presented that "Michael Wood, farmer of Chelsham Court, has stopped up the ancient footway from Slines Hill to Chelsham Church. It starts at Worms Heath, leads through Heath Oaks woodlands and across the Heath to Old Berry. Then through Old Berry Shaw, the corner of Bush Grove, where it joins the other footway from Chelsham Court to the Church. He is ordered to lay the path open before the next court."

1783   Caterham parish register bears the heading "Births, Christenings, & Burials since the first of October 1783, at which time an Act took place imposing a duty of threepence on each."

1888   Caterham Junction railway station was renamed Purley.

1917   The British Red Cross Society and The Order of St John of Jerusalem in England's Roll of Hospitals as at this day listed seven such hospitals in the Bourne Society area, with a total of 204 beds. The largest was at The Red Gables, White Hill, Bletchingley, which had 50 beds.

1940   "Woldingham - The local civilians seem to think that the German Air Force is bent upon wiping out any Canadians, and every time we get a few bombs in this area they blame it on us." (War Diary West Nova Scotia Regiment)

2nd   1749   In Caterham was "Buried by permission of Harvey Acton, Coroner, Samuel Smith, who was killed by a fall from a waggon near the Half Moon in ye Turnpike Road."

1893   "Lovely Day. Croydon Fair. 2 loads of flints to Whiteleafe. Ploughing in 22 acres. Sent 21 lambs to the fair & sold them to Mr Todd for 17/6 each, put into Bank £18.7s.6." (Beech Farm Diaries)

3rd   1548   William Ownstead was fined 2d at Warlingham manor court for selling ale untasted by the Aletaster.

1549   (First name unknown) Harlot was fined 4d for selling underweight bread in Warlingham.

1944   A talk was given to the St Nicholas Youth Fellowship and the Lagham Youth Club by Mr O. Vermulen, a refugee from Belgium who came to England in 1940. He told them about his country, including the fact that although women could vote at municipal elections they had not been given the Parliamentary Franchise (with the exception of women whose husbands were killed in the Great War.) He also said that "England was the only great power that had never invaded Belgium" and "he had great hopes regarding our future cooperation."

4th   1550   William Ownstead was fined at Warlingham manor court for selling beer in "unlicensed and unsealed measures" i.e. in unmarked containers.

1902   At 3.30 p.m. the Ceremony of Laying the Foundation Stone of the Caterham Cottage Hospital took place, with Mr W.Garland Soper laying the stone.

1907   Formation of the Caterham and District Rifle Club, to train British subjects to be "better fitted to serve their Country in the Armed Forces....in the defence of the realm in times of peril."

5th   1325   King Edward II visited the manor house at Bletchingley. The manorial accounts show that, in preparation for his visit, improvements had been made to some of the buildings: "4s 0d for 2,000 flat tiles to roof the bailiff's apartments for the arrival of the king. 4d for 18 corner tiles for the same apartments. 16d for 1 quarter 3 bushels of lime for the same."

1659   At the Quarter Sessions held in Kingston Francis Squire and Robert Poole, who were "Vagrants and goeing vnder the name of Egiptians", failed to appear to answer charges of vagrancy. John Foster, Churchwarden of Limpsfield, had spent £4 14s 8d in apprehending them and was ordered to sell a "Mare and a Pannell" (either a saddle or a saddle-cloth) found in their possession to recoup his costs. The

Constable of Limpsfield was to exact a rate upon the parish's inhabitants to raise the shortfall, or else he would be held in contempt of Court.

6th   1596   The residents of Warlingham were ordered by the manor court to repair the stocks and the archery butts or incur a fine of nine pounds.

1928   The Capitol Cinema opened, in Croydon Road, Caterham. It was built on vacant land at the side of Vigar's old forge. (In 1956 it was refurbished and renamed The Florida, and it finally closed on 13th August 1960, being demolished in 1964.)

1939   "The Chief Education Officer has agreed to my proposal to cultivate land in Schoolgrounds beyond the larch tree plantation." (Kenley Primary School Log Book)

7th   1388   At Coulsdon manor court "Adam Smyth stood at the lord's mercy having been presented by the bailiff for depasturing the common of the lord's tenants in Sladene. (i.e. Standen, later called Standing Lodge, a freehold estate in Coulsdon manor.)

1951   Hubert E. Pounds observed a Blackcap "at close quarters near the western edge of the Titsey plantation. It was moving amongst some elder bushes and consumed a few of the berries with evident relish." The bird is "a singer of a very high order, but the peculiarly abrupt, seemingly unfinished, termination of its remarkably rich and powerful song is a fairly ready means of distinguishing it from the Garden-Warbler."

8th   1342   The Master of the order of St Thomas of Acre, tenant of Taunton in Coulsdon—which belonged to Chertsey Abbey—was charged at the manor court with having made a purpresture or illegal enclosure of land. The court took the purpresture away from him and granted it to John de Redele of Riddlesdown for himself and his heirs. He was already a tenant of Taunton, and was ordered to pay an extra halfpenny rent to the Master for the enclosure, but would actually hold it from the abbot by the performance of the customary services of the manor's tenants.

1395   Thomas de Purlee was fined 2d at Coulsdon manor court for having allowed the king's highway at Longes tenement to become dangerous for lack of repair.

1783   In Chipstead "Mary Hammond, a pauper, interred at ye expense of the parish of Mestham. No Tax duty paid."

1940   "Maj. Bowman's V.D. Clinic at Liskeard. Routine activities. Dull." (The clinic was held every 3 or 4 days. Liskeard was a house in Caterham.) (War Diary B Company, No.5 Field Ambulance, R.C.A.M.C.)

9th   1615   Richard ffysher of Merstham accused Richard Myles of "assaulting him uppon the highwaye and for violentlye riding uppon him with his horse whereby he is grievously hurte in his body." (Bostock Fuller J.P.)

1943   "Little Selkirk, Caterham - The invasion of Caterham, Surrey, took place this morning and the place is now occupied by 4 Med. Regt. R.C.A." (A French Canadian regiment) "The instalement of the unit into its new luxurious billets took very little time. Soon after supper, the town was swarming with our boys, making a preliminary reconnaissance. In view of language difficulties experienced by most of them it is surprising to see how quickly they can get around." (War Diary 4 Med. Regt. R.C.A.)

10th 1617   William fflynte was bound over to appear at the next Quarter Sessions charged with "resisting and assaulting John Dodd highe Constable of the lower halfe hundred of Tanridg in executing and doeing his office." (Bostock Fuller J.P.)

1739   In Merstham church "William Smith Widower and Hannah Woollmer both of the parish of Wandsworth were (after three days' waiting that I might be satisfied of some doubts) married by Licence."

1896   "Beautiful day. Men digging potatoes in the field. Palmer thatching stack. Stag turned out at Worms Heath." (Beech Farm Diaries)

11th 1863   At 6.30 p.m. the Caterham Congregational Church held its first assembly, over a carpenter's shop.

1940   "21.46: Message from Kenley Police re UXBs near Farleigh Court - advised Police that site was in Coulsdon & Purley." (Red to White Log Book of Caterham and Warlingham U.D. Report and Control Centre)

12th 1546   In Warlingham Peter Hammond, of Croydon, was fined for illegally selling beer and William Ownsted, a baker, was fined 2d for selling underweight bread.

13th 1840   *The London Gazette* reported that the parish of Coulsdon was added to the Metropolitan Police District.

1901   The first fatal motor car accident on the Brighton Road occurred at Smitham Bottom. *The Motor Car Journal* reported "at Croydon Edgar Cundy of South Norwood was summoned for furiously driving a motor car....The police evidence as to speed was conflicting, various estimates ranging from 16 to 153 mph."

1915   The zeppelin raid reported below (14th) was also remembered by Maurice Cooke, who, as a small boy, heard his neighbour, Mr Cliffe (a member of the Purley Special Constabulary), say that it was "so low he could have thrown his truncheon at it."

14th 1915   "A zeppelin raid last night. Many of the children and their parents have been up all the night. One zeppelin was seen over Kenley and the noise of the exploding bombs over Croydon was plainly seen and heard, particularly from Kenley and Riddlesdown. Most of the inhabitants were awakened by the noise and were up and about. All the children in a state of excitement all day.(Kenley National School Log Book)

15th 1935 David Seth-Smith gave a Lantern Lecture entitled "The Zoo and its Inmates" to the Caterham Literary Society. He was Curator of Mammals and Birds at London Zoo and was known to a wide B.B.C. listenership as the "Zoo Man."

1941 "Woldingham Surrey - A meeting of all Officers at Bn. H.Q. heard a very interesting talk by Lieut D.W.McAdam, who has just returned from the new school of Tank Hunting. This new type of warfare appeals to everyone, although it is highly unorthodox, and rough and tumble." (War Diary West Nova Scotia Regiment)

16th 1615 A warrant was issued for the arrest of Raffe Monke (probably of Bletchingley) and others "for playeing at cards in his house yesterday being the sabbath day." (Bostock Fuller J.P.)

1987 Surrey was struck by its worst storm since 1703. One result of this "hurricane" was the devastation wreaked amongst the tree population: roughly ten percent of the county's trees were damaged in some way. In the parks and open spaces in the Borough of Croydon, which include Coulsdon Common, Riddlesdown and Farthing Downs, 70,000 trees were blown down, as were another 5,000 which had stood in the streets.

17th 1575 At Sanderstead manor court it was presented that "John Woodstock unjustly and wrongfully went on to the common land of the demesne called Saundersted Heth with his pigs, causing loss to the Tenants. And he has a day to cease this under penalty of 10s." At the same court an order was made "to distrain Lady Anne Dannet for her rent: 20s is owed in unpaid arrears for the past two years."

1939 "Air Raid warning (Yellow) received at 1.55 p.m. Children all in shelter in 2 minutes. 'All Clear' signal received at 3 p.m." (Kenley Primary School Log Book)

18th 1941 "Woldingham - During the early hours of the evening it seemed that our area was about to be 'blitzed' and for two hours the buildings shook and rattled from bombs and A.A. gun-fire. The only damage was caused on Station Road, where a bomb blew trees and part of a cutting into the road. 'A' Coy turned out and cleared the road in short order." (War Diary West Nova Scotia Regiment)

19th 1939 "Owing to shelters being too wet for occupation, school was dismissed at 11.30 a.m. for the rest of the day. Dinner children remained under supervision of Headmaster." (Kenley Primary School Log Book)

1945 A Royal Canadian Air Force Dakota, KG459, of 435 Transport Squadron, nose-dived into a front garden in Mitchley Avenue, Purley. It appeared to develop engine trouble shortly after taking off from Croydon. Three Canadian crew members were killed, and Frank Moore, an R.A.F. sergeant died the following day. There were no civilian casualties. *(Plate XIX)*

1977 The Miller Centre in Caterham Valley was formally opened by David Ennals M.P., Secretary of State for Social Services.

20th 1410 Richard atte Water was fined 3s 4d at Farleigh manor court "because he was a rebel, and refused to obey the lord's official minister and carry out his work on the lord's land."

1574 The residents of Sanderstead and Warlingham agreed to divide the common land at Riddlesdown between them, to settle a long standing dispute.

1821 "Poor old Dame Miller, who had worked for our family for over twenty years, fell into a pond in her garden and was drowned." (Diary of Mrs William Jolliffe of Merstham)

1939 "Children assembled at 8.55 a.m. but as the shelters were still very wet School was dismissed without registers being marked." (Kenley Primary School Log Book)

21st 1853 First mention of a railway to Caterham in correspondence between the London Brighton and South Coast and the South Eastern Railways.

1982 A "Night of Music" was held at the United Reform Church in Purley, presented by the Croydon Salvation Army Band and Songsters, to raise money for the Ionozon Therapy Unit needed by the Purley Memorial Hospital.

22nd 1908 "Two degrees of Frost this morning & biting N.E. wind blowing. I notice it nips some of the children. From observation of late it seems to me some of our children do not appear to be so well clad, shod & fed as formerly." (Kenley National School Log Book)

1940 Bletchingley Report Post recorded an H.E. bomb dropped at 21.48 on Sandhills Farm, Bletchingley: "Cow shed demolished. Farm buildings severely damaged. 4 cows killed. 4 cattle injured. Bletchingley & Oxted Rescue Parties sent. Veterinary Surgeon informed."

23rd 1413 At the Coulsdon manor court "Walter atte Halle begged leave of the lord to marry Joan, widow of Walter Redele, and for this permission he paid one shilling, the customary fine for such a licence."

1983 As part of the preparations to celebrate Chaldon's novocentenary (900 years since its mention in Domesday Book) the cleaning out and restoration of the Court Farm Pond was due to start on this weekend. The work was to be done by the British Trust of Conservation Volunteers, assisted by Chaldon Venture Scouts and others.

24th 1845 An auction was held at Ledgers House in Chelsham of all the Household Furniture, Contents, livestock, agricultural produce etc. Items varied from squirrel cage to man-trap, from exercising horse to Bay draught horse, from Japanned slipper bath to broad-wheel dung cart, from a dwarf cupboard to a six foot six patent mangle, from 8 coloured engravings of "The Quorn Hunt" to about 800 volumes of books.

25th 1927 Members of the Whyteleafe Cricket Club and friends held their first festive gathering since cricket had been stopped by the Great War. It "was held in the Church Hall, and a pleasing feature was the presence of many ladies....Altogether a party of about sixty sat down to the well-set-out tables." There was musical and humorous entertainment provided by London and local artistes. *(Weekly Press and County Post)*

1945 The Canadian crew of the crashed Dakota KG459 (see 19th October 1945)—F.H. Seaman (pilot), G.A.McIntyre (co-pilot) and E.J. Shaw (navigator)—were buried at Brookwood.

26th 1586 At Chelsham manor court it was reported "on oath that Jocasta Pather, wife of Simon Pather, who held of the lord of this manor for her life time certain free lands called Bedlested died since the last court and so there falls due to the lord a relief of 24s 7½d. And that John Bassett is the next heir and is of full age. He is present and seeks permission and did fealty."

1940 "An all night raid....H.Es and incendiaries were distributed in many parts of the Urban District and beyond in Farleigh, Woldingham and Chelsham, the whole area being illuminated. There was a good deal of machine gun firing by the raiders. Although the attack was so long and the damage was heavy, no casualties were reported." *(Weekly Press and County Post)*

27th 1913 "Our Diocesan, the Right Rev. Dr Burge, Bishop of Southwark, visited the School this morning, accompanied by the Vicar. He was very interested in the work of the school, & was particularly pleased with the children's handwork, & the drawing & colour work of the senior scholars. He gave an encouraging address to the children & said he should carry away with him very pleasant recollections of his visit to the school." (Kenley National School Log Book)

1914 "Admitted two Belgian refugee boys; they were in the last boat to leave Antwerp. Gustave Ganses & Jean Geurickse." (Kenley National School Log Book)

28th 1404 At Farleigh manor court "William atte Parke brings a charge against John Bryan that he broke into the lord's private land and there stole heron chicks valued at 3s 4d causing damage assessed at £1 0s 0d. John Bryan admitted his guilt and was fined 4d."

1983 The Bourne Society held its Autumn Meeting at Kenley Memorial Hall, and heard a lecture by Richard Elliott on the history of clocks. At the meeting the "bookstall was present, though untroubled."!

29th 1615 "Raffe Monnke of Bletchingley was bound over to appear at the next Croydon Quarter Sessions to answere his offence for keeping unlawfull playe and games in his house heretofore." (Bostock Fuller J.P.)

1935 The Caterham Literary Society was lectured to by Miss Wilhelmina Stitch, who was "well known as a lecturer and as the writer of 'The Fragrant Minute'." Her subject was "My Discovery of America."

30th 1913 The Lord Bishop of Southwark performed the ceremony of the cutting of the first sod, at St Andrew's Church in Coulsdon.

1940 At Caterham and Warlingham Report and Control Centre three Air Raid Messages Red (i.e. Warnings) were received at 11.45, 15.46 and 19.04. A.R.M. White (i.e. All Clears) were received at 12.58, 16.57, and at 03.45 the following morning. Also "16.35: Police report that suspected UXB, 25 Annes Walk, has exploded" and "22.02 Surrey Control notify reports of new enemy missiles. Copy to A.R.P.O. All Divisional Wardens, Police, Fire Brigade, Casualty & Engineer services informed." (Red to White Log Book)

31st 1601 An Indenture of this date records the conveyance by Sir Oliphe Leigh of Addington to John Whitgift, Archbishop of Canterbury, of the manor of Croham with all its lands and properties in Sanderstead and Croydon. Sir Oliphe retained that part of the manor which was in Addington parish and two acres in Selsdon.

1867 The Caterham Vestry Minutes contain a report on the Godstone Workhouse as follows: "Irrespective of Tramps, the inmates are generally the sick, the aged, the infirm and children without parents. Able bodied paupers happily do not often seek admission."

1912 At 3.30 p.m. F.B. Malim, master of Haileybury College, addressed the Women's Diocesan Association of the Caterham Deanery on the subject of "The Value of Austerity in Education." Tea followed at 4.30 p.m.

1913 "Three children are excluded for Whooping Cough, & colds are very prevalent amongst the children." (Kenley National School Log Book)

1936 Members of Warlingham Ratepayers' Association met representatives of Surrey County Council in an attempt to prevent a school being built at Wapses Lodge, Caterham. They organised a campaign "Stop the Death School", because of worries about building a school so close to the proposed new by-pass.

NOVEMBER

1st 1615 John Hammond of Chelsham was bound over to be of good behaviour until the next Croydon General Sessions where he should be charged with "killing a dogge of William Woodes which did drawe dry foote after which tyme he had great losses, and also for kylling conyes with a stonebowe in the grounds of (Peter) Obberd." (Bostock Fuller J.P.)

1904 The Caterham and District Gas Company "received a letter from Mr Nichols of the Rose and Crown" complaining that the Company had caused the "Bourne flow to flood his land. Following one of the Company's oldest customs, the secretary was instructed to take no notice of the letter, beyond a formal acknowledgement of it."

1913 Death of "Poor Old Ike", an African ape, a veteran of the Boer War and the Ladysmith siege brought back as a pet by a soldier and subsequently kept at Gardner's Pleasure Resort on Riddlesdown. After his death he was stuffed and exhibited in a glass case. *(Plate XX & XXI)*

1943 "Rain. This seems a very damp valley." (War Diary 2nd Canadian H.A.A. Regiment, based in Caterham)

2nd 1283 "Blechingley Fair held this day - originally granted on 1st October 1283 to Gilbert de Clare, Earl of Gloucester, for three days viz on the Eve, Feast and Morn of All Saints." (Footnote to Bostock Fuller J.P.)

1412 At Coulsdon manor court Thomas Purlee was fined 2d "for having obstructed the highway at Collysdon Strete by the height of a hedge which was due to the omission of lopping, as Thomas should have done by custom."

3rd 1458 At the Court of Thomas Cooke, lord of the manor of Chelsham Watvyles, it was presented that Roger Derannt of Limpsfield, a butcher, did on several occasions break into and enter closes and lands of Thomas Cooke and "with many other wrong doers and breakers of the King's peace, took 20 of the lord's rabbits worth 6s 8d."

1825 "Sir William Jolliffe had a bad fall hunting early in the day. His horse fell again at Smytham Bottom and died in ten minutes." (Diary of Mrs William Jolliffe of Merstham)

1855 A dinner was held at the *White Hart* in Godstone to celebrate the return of Captain C. H. Turner, hero of the Crimea and grandson of C.H. Turner, magistrate, of Rook's Nest.

4th 1539 Henry VIII granted to Sir John Gresham "the manor of Sanderstead, lands in Tandridge and rents in Chelsham."

1614 "I sent Thomas Dunstane to the House of Correction taken at Blechinglye ffayre drunke and quarrelling and he said he had noe dwelling and he accused Arthur ffylpott for killing one Richard Curteys at Groombridg ffaire about a yeare since." (Bostock Fuller J.P.)

1912 "8 wild geese travelling in V formation passed over Warlingham flying in a westerly direction." (Arthur Beadell's Nature Notes)

1940   "A solo bomber dropped bombs in Chaldon-road, where several shops and houses were damaged. Whilst going to the aid of some children a tradesman was killed and other persons were injured. The enemy also opened fire with a machine gun upon some children just leaving the Council School. Two of the boys were seriously injured and one of them died in hospital." *(Weekly Press and County Post)*

5th   1739   Bletchingley churchwardens "pd. the Ringers for Powder Plott 5s."

1936   Edgar J. March Esq. gave the Caterham Literary Society a Lantern and Cinematograph Lecture entitled "Building the Mammoth Liner 'Queen Mary'." The accompanying film showed "the ceremony at the launch of the ship by H.M. the Queen, filmed from every angle."

1977   The Caterham Players presented the first play at the Miller Centre—a comedy, *All in Good Time*, by Bill Naughton. Directed by Dorothy Miles, the play was on from 5th to 12th November.

6th   1914   "Instead of the usual Nature Lesson this afternoon, children in Stds 3, 4, 5, 6 & 7 were taken for a Nature Ramble after playtime by Miss F.A. Smith (Goldsmiths' T. College) over Riddlesdown and round the Farm. They had a particularly good view of an Aeroplane that was flying over & which went through some interesting manoeuvres overhead. The abundance of berries this year of all kinds is remarkable and quite a feature of the landscape." (Kenley National School Log Book)

7th   1725   Coulsdon parish register records the marriage of John Matthews and Elizabeth Wicken. A note has been interlined in a different hand as follows: "1758
       <u>1725</u> John Matthews, Clark, has been
       <u> 33</u> married so long."

1825   "Paid Nathaniel Brooke 1 Day for cleaning the Church Windows. 2s.0d." (Caterham Churchwardens' Accounts)

8th   1886   "Admitted James Blann. This boy and his brother & sister put in an appearance at this School, when opened first, for one half day, but being bad behaved children, they thought the discipline here would not be to their liking, so they left & went back to Riddlesdown School. They have not paid any School money there for sometime, and to escape payment have now turned up at this School again, & being in this Parish I am of course obliged to admit them. James Blann is very backward in Arithmetic and his writing is disgraceful. He has been allowed to get into the habit of writing left handed and now it is impossible to get him out of it. Emma Blann is also very backward for her age." (Kenley National School Log Book)

9th   1879   The luxurious country house built in the 17th century by Sir Robert Clayton in Marden Park was destroyed by fire, partly because of the lack of available water. (In 1677 John Evelyn had remarked that the site lacked running water, as had a later tenant, William Wilberforce.) Only the stables survived. It was tenanted at the time by Arthur Andrews, a City, East India and China merchant. *(Plate XXII)*

10th 1619 "Michaell Smythe of Blechinglye" was bound over on condition that "he shall not resorte to any house of unlawfull games nor shall hereafter use or playe at any unlawfull games." (Bostock Fuller J.P.)

11th 1445 A pardon was issued to "Thomas Basset of Cullesdon, co. Surrey 'husbondman', for not appearing before the" Justices of the Kings Bench "to answer Thomas Hever touching a debt of 10L." (Calendar of Patent Rolls)

1917 A Royal Flying Corps biplane crashed in a lane off Hall Hill in Oxted. The pilot was saved from serious injury by the wings getting caught in the hedges on either side of the lane.

1993 Gamekeepers on the Beddlestead estate in Chelsham caught four poachers red-handed "as they stowed the dead birds, together with three catapults used to poach them, into their get-away van." The gamekeepers had kept watch for about an hour and had heard "cracking, then flapping of wings, then a thud as of something hitting the ground, and they saw four men firing." 18 pheasants were killed and two more had to be destroyed. One of the men, who appeared before the court separately, was fined £100, ordered to pay £105.75 compensation and £35 costs, and it was ordered that his catapult should be destroyed. *(Croydon Advertiser)*

12th 1545 Sir Thomas Cawarden of Bletchingley led twelve armed men to take over Abbots Wood in Caterham by force and enclose it to form part of his deer park.

1906 "Refused admission to Mary, Percy, Edwin and William Higgs: school full. It is very hard that these children should have to run about the streets, owing to lack of school accommodation." (Maple Road Junior (Mixed) School, Whyteleafe)

13th 1810 At 12 noon the auction took place of "That distinguished and elegant Freehold Mansion called Selsdon House, delightfully situated on a fine eminence, which commands extensive and beautiful prospects over the county of Surrey, in the centre of a fine sporting country, abounding with game." The house had two wings, a colonnade in front, double coach houses, stabling for eight horses, pleasure grounds, ornamental lodge, adjoining new built farmhouse & associated buildings including an octagon corn mill, stabling for 20 horses, eight cottages plus 900 acres all ring-fenced & tithe-free.

14th 1732 In Merstham the marriage took place of "Joseph Benge & Betty Liew. It is to be remembered that the Bans were publicly forbid in the church by ----- Morphew spinster of this parish but upon her being then publickly told from the Desk how she must proceed according to the Rubrick, she was advised it seems by some to take another method to hinder this man's marriage & prove herself with child by him before Justice Payton tho' in the end it appeared she was not."

1736 A Merstham Vestry meeting resolved "that Mr Henry Stowel have a months time allowed him to bring a true and legal Certificate to this Vestry from the Clergyman that married him & where he is to be found before we give him trouble in Drs Commons." Also "that Mr Robert Ward have till Xstmass next allowed him to bring a certificate from the parish he belongs to that he nor his Children ever become chargeable to this Parish."

1892 "Palmer mending gaps after the fox-hunters. Started for Kingston Fair but the Pony fell & cut her knees so that I had to come back." (Beech Farm Diaries)

15th 1574 John Read of Tandridge was appointed Sheriff of Surrey and Sussex.

1904 A Bazaar was held at the Public Hall in Caterham on 15th and 16th November. It was on behalf of the Church of England Waifs' and Strays' Society and St Mary's Church Magazine reported that it "proved a signal success. The sum to be handed over to the Society will amount to over £200."

16th 1943 "Little Selkirk, Caterham - All available personnel take a route march down to the Capitol Cinema in Caterham for the showing of 2 training films: 'The Louse' and 'Next-of-kin'. The latter, being an excellent film on security, makes one think twice before talking." (War Diary 4th Medium Regiment R.C.A.)

1947 Dedication of a memorial window in Chaldon Church to Lance Corporal John Pennington Harman V.C. (See 20th June 1944) He was the son of Martin Coles Harman. (See 5th December 1954)

17th 1215 Roland de Oxted, who took the baronial side against King John, had his lands "committed to his Oxted neighbour and great royal servant, Hugh de Nevill." (Surrey Eyre)

1616 Tho. Payce of Chelsham was bound over until the next Quarter Sessions charged with "begetting of Grace Mosle with childe and for diverse other misdemeanours and ill behaviour." (Bostock Fuller J.P.)

18th 1675 Harman Atwood officially established the Warlingham Almshouses. He named seven trustees and appointed the Vicar as local manager. Two of the almshouses were allotted to the poor of Warlingham, one to Sanderstead and one to Chelsham. *(Plate XXIII)*

1899 At 3 p.m. a Jumble Sale was held, "for parish purposes", at the Board Schools in Caterham Valley. Tickets were one penny each, and were obtainable from Mrs Barber. (St Mary's Church Magazine)

1904 A later edition of the same magazine recorded that "a very interesting and instructive Lantern Entertainment was very kindly provided by Mr Warren at the Parish Hall. The subject was 'Gigantic Littleness', illustrating the power of the microscope, rendering visible those minute objects which are almost invisible to the naked eye."

19th 1291 William de Lisle of Cambridgeshire confessed to the king's justices on 24th Nov. that on 19th he had taken part in the robbing of Walter of Codestone (Godstone). His share of the booty—which had been linen and woollen cloths, horses, jewels and other goods—had been one mark. He gave away his confederates, including Little Jack of Edenbridge. (Coroners' Rolls)

1401 The rent paid by Robert Kynsolde for one house and nine acres of land at Beddlestead in Chelsham was 20d a year, payable quarterly, and two ploughshares, two chickens and 20 eggs.

1616 "I sent a warrant to Blechinglye and Hoorne to serch for goods stollen from Richard Betts, and they brought ----- Toller with a goose which he said he stole from Rose Harling, and I charged the Constable to laye him by the heeles all night and to bring him again next morning. He brake the stocks and ran away." (Bostock Fuller J.P.)

20th 1817 "Mr William got up before 6 a.m. and went off to Town with Mr Paul. Mr Jolliffe and Mr Inglis hunted and killed three foxes." (Diary of Mrs William Jolliffe of Merstham)

1885 "The Kenley Horticultural & Cottage Gardener's Society, by permission of the School Managers, held a Chrysanthemum Show in the School room today, in aid of School funds. No School all day in Consequence." (Kenley National School Log Book)

21st 1736 The baptism took place in Warlingham of "Martha the d. of James Anderson (si mulieri Credas*) and Sara Comport." (*'if you believe the woman')

1955 Mr Baedeker U.E. Ramage wrote to the Coulsdon and Purley Chief Librarian recalling that "In my schooldays and as a young man, I spent many pleasant days, even haymaking, at the Farm known as Purley Oaks....I believe I still have a print of the interior of the old barn and showing The Gibbet Post which originally stood I believe by the Royal Oak." (See 30th December 1955) *(Plate XXIV)*

22nd 1761 In Merstham "William Midgley (an old Soldier) from the Poor House was Buried."

1903 The greatest Bourne flow for many years began on this day, below the *Rose and Crown.* By 22nd December it had become a visible stream running through Purley and it did not cease until 3rd June 1904.

23rd 1630 In Sanderstead "A Poore woman brought sicke to the towne (from Croydon) Nov 22 & dyinge ye night following was Buried."

       1978   A full meeting of Tandridge District Council approved by 21 votes to 13 that No.1 Stafford Road in Caterham should be used for an East Surrey Museum, subject to satisfactory plans and reports. (See 22nd Feb 1979 and 10th May 1980)

24th   1904   The Directors of the Caterham Gas Company decided, at a Board Meeting, that "all the leading hands and fitters were to be allowed to visit the Gas Exhibition at Earls Court. Their fare and tickets of admission were to be paid for them, and each man was to receive 2s to pay for his tea and supper."

       1946   The 'Oxted and Limpsfield Men's Meeting' was given a lecture in the Working Men's Club in Oxted entitled "Modern Man in Search of a Soul" by Michael Tippett. Meetings were held at 7.45 p.m. every Sunday and "The important topics of the day are introduced by a Speaker and afterwards left open for questions or discussion." The 'Brotherhood' or 'Fellowship of Men' as it is variously described also assisted in Social Work and ran a Benevolent Fund. At the bottom of the Programme is the legend: "If you Smoke, bring your Pipe along with you....and bring a Friend too."

25th   1935   Prince Arthur of Connaught, son of Queen Victoria, opened the Boys' Club in Chipstead Valley Road. *(Plate XXV)*

       1935   A Monday—commencing at 1.30 p.m. today and showing for six days, the programme at Caterham's Capitol Cinema was *The 39 Steps* starring Robert Donat and Madeline Carrol. It was described as "the finest British film of the year."

26th   1706   Tatsfield parish register records that "John, the child which was found at More-House was buried." (See 16th Sept 1705)

       1909   "A very old friend visited the School this morning - H.W. Vardon Esq. He was one of the School Managers from the opening of the School in 1885 till he left the neighbourhood 9 years ago. He used to be a firm & consistent friend to the children, though only a very few in the School remember him now." (Kenley National School Log Book)

       1928   Ward's Croydon Directory records that today the Coulsdon Council sent "a protest to the Air Ministry against the increase of stunt and low flying of air planes."

27th   1521   Henry VIII stayed at Bletchingley Place to greet Cardinal Wolsey on his return from an embassy to France.

       1576   Martin Gumyns of Nutfield, a collier, stole 10 pairs of shoes (worth 10s) and 17d in money from John Merchaunt at Godstone. He was indicted for grand larceny at Croydon Assizes, found guilty, but allowed clergy.

       1870   "Twelve geese were stolen from the premises of J. Scott Esq. of Rook's Nest, Oxted. Police Constables 95 and 55 were actively engaged the whole of Monday to find the perpetrators of so gross an act and there is every possibility of the guilty parties being brought to justice." *(Croydon Advertiser)*

28th 1613 Warrant issued for Robert Allingham of Nutfield accused of "stealing a swine and akernes in a bagg from Allens wydowe" but she "would not pursue yt as felonye....after muche reasoning they lett him goe." (Bostock Fuller J.P.)

1892 "The places of the teachers who are absent owing to Scarlet Fever are temporarily filled with temporary monitresses. Through the kindness of her parents Edith Woodgate, a 4th St. girl, is filling the place of one. I find that some of the Kenley gentry, as usual in any outbreak of sickness here, are scared, and have ordered some parents not to send their children to school otherwise the fathers must give up their work. In other cases, where the mothers take in washing they have been ordered to either keep their Children at home or to have the work taken from them. There is no need for them to be so frightened." (Kenley National School Log Book)

29th 1754 A letter written on this date and included in *The Travels Through England of Dr Richard Pococke* refers to some local earthworks: "At Bottle Hill is a square rampart and a single ditch, and another on a hill near Katheram, which place is directly west of Westram."

1839 The steward of Chipstead manor, a Reigate lawyer, gave notice that on this date, a Friday, at 11 a.m., there would be a meeting of the manor Court at the *Star* in Hooley Lane. (The *Star* was demolished in 1978 to remove a slight bend in the Brighton Road.)

30th 1912 "An abnormal crop of beech nuts has attracted large flocks of wood pigeons which are feeding under the trees. Fieldfares commenced feeding on haws. Rabbits stripping the bark from the underwood. This is most unusual as we have not, so far, had any severe wintry weather." (Arthur Beadell's Nature Notes)

DECEMBER

1st 1377 The Bishop of Winchester sent an order to the rectors of Bletchingley and Chaldon telling them to announce the excommunication of malefactors who had stolen timber and other wood from the lands of John de Uvedale of Titsey.

1886 J.N. Crawford, the famous Surrey cricketer, was born at Cane Hill, where his father was chaplain for 35 years. In 1905 he became the youngest man to play for England. *(Plate XXVI)*

1909 "The Girls attended this afternoon at the Roke Centre for a Course of 10 lessons in Laundry Work 1.30-4. As we only knew for certain that they were to attend, a few minutes before 1.30, they had to rush off through torrents of rain to get there on time." (Kenley National School Log Book)

2nd 1890 A Little Auk "was caught in a state of extreme exhaustion on a pond at Godstone. Its weight was three and a half ounces, and it was preserved by Mr. C Reeves, the Reigate taxidermist." (Hubert E. Pounds.)

1910 "The girls are sorry the Laundry Course is completed. They appear to have done good work. They asked me to give them something to get up for me to show what they could do. I gave them some dirty collars, & they returned them to me got up very nicely, quite equal to good laundry works." (Kenley National School Log Book)

3rd 1908 "The School Attendance Officer visited this morning. Had a conversation with him with regard to helping some of the parents to provide their children with good boots. Mr William is interesting himself very much in this matter. Gave him the names of certain families whom I thought stood in need of some assistance. Although poverty may not be so apparent with us as in some schools I am afraid some of our Parents are hard put to this winter & I should be extremely pleased if they could be assisted for the sake of the children, though I am afraid in some cases, the mothers are the chief sufferers as they deny themselves for the sake of the little ones." (Kenley National School Log Book—follow-up to 22nd October 1908)

1933 The Godstone Dr Barnardo's Homes Young Helpers League held their Box-opening at Leigh Place, with their President, Mrs Lines, performing the ceremony. It "was very well attended although it was such a cold day. Everybody had a very happy afternoon. After tea all took part in Competitions while the boxes were opened and the contents counted. Miss Chavasse, the organising representative of the League, came from Stepney and gave a very interesting account of life in the Homes, and then presented ten silver badges to members who had qualified for them. The total collected in the Boxes was £22, which was a satisfactory increase on last year's total and 14 new members were enrolled." (Godstone Parish Magazine)

4th 1894 A parish meeting was held in the school in Chelsham "to elect the appointment of way wardens, allotments and the distribution of parochial charities. The attendance was only fair." (Chelsham and Warlingham Parish Magazine)

5th 1954 Death of Martin Coles Harman, one of six sons and five daughters born to William Harman and Florence (née Coles) of Caterham. With his father he built Deans Place in Chaldon, and then bought a seven acre field, also in Chaldon, which he presented to the National Trust for the use of the inhabitants as a sportsfield. He asked that the field should forever be known as Six Brothers Field. He also bought Lundy Island in the Bristol Channel and had six granite boulders from there transferred to the Chaldon field and arranged in a circle, to commemorate the six brothers.

6th 1577 Richard Basset of Chelsham, yeoman, with six other yeomen and a tailor from Cobham, a yeoman from Broomfield and another from Westerham (both in Kent), were indicted at Croydon Assizes for riotous assembly, poaching and assault. They were accused of having broken into the grounds of Chelsham Court, which belonged to John Lambe, on this date. They took six rabbits with nets and assaulted Denise, the wife of John Lambe. (The verdict is unknown)

1915 Death of Walter Smith, aged 62. He had been headmaster of Kenley National School since its opening in 1885, and had kept the detailed School Log Books which have been quoted so often in this volume. There is a brass tablet to his memory in All Saints Church, Kenley.

7th 1796 In order to provide for the Defence of the Realm Croydon Vestry considered "the most speedy and effectual means of raising Nine Men for the Service of his Majesty's Army appointed to be raised by the Parish of Croydon in Conjunction with the Parishes of Sanderstead and Addington." They "ordered that the Churchwardens and Overseers of the poor of this Parish do immediately make a Rate or Assessment upon all and every the Occupiers of Lands Tenements Tythes and Hereditaments within the said parish towards raising and paying the Bounties to Nine Men....at Six Pence in the pound Rent."

1821 "William Jolliffe comes of age. Church bells rang all day. Flags were hung out on the house and church. Every poor family in Merstham had meat, bread and a bushel of coals. Presents were given to all the servants." (Diary of Mrs William Jolliffe of Merstham)

1940 "Most of the young Officers of the Unit enjoyed a Ground Hockey Match this afternoon with the young people of Woldingham, on the Woldingham Cricket Pitch. Several of the Officers attended a very enjoyable dance tonight at the home of Miss Dianna Courtney of Woldingham." (War Diary West Nova Scotia Regiment)

8th 1440 "John Godfrey, son of William Godfrey of Caterham, who had been apprenticed to John Ropkyn, saddler, for a term of ten years, was exonerated from his apprenticeship on the ground that his master had not instructed him in the trade nor provided him with necessaries." (Calendar of Plea and Memoranda Rolls)

1940 "Woldingham - All Guards were warned to be on the alert tonight for two men driving a stolen car. They are believed to be enemy agents." (War Diary West Nova Scotia Regiment)

9th 1924 The sale was held of "The Mill House" in Warlingham: "The property adjoins the 'Leather Bottle' close to The Green. It consists of a spacious shop, a comfortable dwelling house, a cottage (formerly the bake house), a timber yard, useful farm buildings and about 10½ acres of land. Gas, water and electric light are available."

10th 1614 "William Bersytho a saylor was broughte before me for stealing Glovers wyves smocke which he confessed and she hathe it agayne and I sent him to the gaole by Rumnye the Borsholder of Godstone and he suffered him to escape." (Bostock Fuller J.P.)

11th 1554 Anne of Cleves wrote an angry letter to Sir Thomas Cawarden requesting his overdue rent for Bletchingley Place.

1940 The Y.M.C.A., which had arranged to take over the Imperial Ice Rink in Purley for the use of the Canadian soldiers stationed locally, both for ice hockey and pleasure skating, reported that by today 200 men were playing hockey there every day. Also, on Saturday and Sunday afternoons, there were 500-600 skaters.

12th 1679 Francis Coventry Esq., a J.P. for Surrey, certified that today "Catherine Wilson came before him & made affidavit in the presence of Richard Mose and Mary Curd, that the corpse of Elizabeth the wife of Richard Mose was not put in, wrapt, wound up, or buried in any thing, but what was made of sheepswooll onely; neither was the coffin lined or faced with any thing. The corpse of the abovesaid Elizabeth Mose was buried the 6 day of Decemb. 1679" in Farleigh churchyard.

13th 1892 "I, Fanny Webb, Certificated Mistress, took charge of this school. 72 children presented themselves for admission, of whom 40 are infants (19 in St.I and 13 in St.II - several in St.II are 12-13 yrs of age & in St.I 10, 11, 12, 13.) Elizabeth Bell aged 13 has assisted with the infants. (Log Book of the Board School in Maple Road, Whyteleafe)

1928 The newly formed Rotary Club of Coulsdon achieved distinction by winning the Attendance Trophy for the District with an average of 97.5%.

14th 1895 "Beautiful day, frosty. Both men at plough in Fusfield. Began to give hay to sheep. Fox hounds all over the place. Mr Eastby here shooting - shot 12 larks 4 rabbits & a pheasant." (Beech Farm Diaries)

1991 The 'Blanchman's Farm Community Wildlife Area' project included a two day archaeological excavation starting today which established that the foundations of the 17/18th century farm buildings still remain barely below the present ground surface. (The earliest known documentary reference to a farm of this name is in 1584.)

15th 1904 The Croydon Gas Company did not wish to take over any private wars and on this date the Directors of the Caterham Gas Company had to agree "that this Company should subscribe £50 towards the cost of constructing a culvert on the Rose & Crown public property subject to Mr Helps' approval." (See 1st Nov 1904)

16th 1880 *The Times* carried the following advertisement: "Asylum for Fatherless Children, Reedham, near Croydon.—Orphans of both sexes are admitted from early infancy and retained till 15 years of age. 300 are now in the asylum. There is no endowment. Annual Subscriptions and Donations are earnestly solicited, and will be thankfully received by the Bankers, Messrs Barclay, Bevan & Co. or by the Secretary, Mr George Stancliff." *(Plate XXVII)*

1917 The 1st Battalion (Croydon) Surrey Volunteer Training Corps (which later became part of the 1st Volunteer Battalion The Queen's Royal West Surrey Regiment) completed "the construction of a portion of the Outer London Defences at Willey Farm, Caterham and Aldercombe." The task had begun on 20th September 1915 and had taken 90,000 hours to carry out. (From 1914 until March 1917 the Volunteers had had to provide all their own equipment, uniform etc. at their own expense, the only item being issued to each man by the Government being a red brassard bearing the letters G.R. (Georgius Rex) which led to their nickname of 'Gorgeous Wrecks'.) (See also 20th Feb 1915 and 8th March 1915) *(Plate XXVIII)*

17th 1886 William Longhurst, a 17 year old labourer, was admitted to the Caterham Cottage Hospital suffering from the bite of a rabid dog, according to the hospital records. He was not discharged until 4th March 1887.

18th 1928 In Chelsham "The annual distribution of the Kelly Bequest Bread Tickets took place on Sunday December 18th. The service was well attended."

1928 The Carol Service "was an enormous success, also a most hearty and inspiring service." (Chelsham and Warlingham Parish Magazine)

1940 "Caterham 19.00 - A concert for the unit is given in CATERHAM School by the Canadian Legion." (War Diary Royal 22e Regiment C.A.S.F.)

19th 1912 "House Sparrows with nesting material renovating old nests for roosting purposes." (Arthur Beadell's Nature Notes)

1915 2nd Lieutenant G.P. Allen (of the 3/4th Battalion The Queen's Royal West Surrey Regiment) "the son of Mr Councillor Francis Allen, of Croydon, was fatally injured, to the great sorrow of his comrades, with whom he was deservedly popular, while attending a course of bombing at Marden Park." He died 2 days later in Caterham Cottage Hospital. *(Plate XXIX)*

20th 1899   The Balance Sheet of the Old Surrey Hounds Slate Club, in Godstone, recorded that during the year they had paid out £41 15s 10d in Sick Pay to members and £5 17s 6d towards the funerals of two members. The remaining balance of £62 8s 11d was to be shared out between the 77 current members—each one to receive 16s 2d, with 4s 1d left over.

21st 1612   John Bassett was attacked in Chelsham by Thomas Glover of West Wickham, John Farrant of Downe and John Glover of Cudham, all yeomen. Thomas Glover struck him on the back with a hop pole, inflicting injuries from which he died on 26th January 1613. They were all indicted for murder at Southwark Assizes, but were found not guilty.

1904   St Thomas' Day. In Chelsham Church a service was held in accordance with "The Kelly Bequest. Needless to say we had a large congregation. About two hundred loaves of bread were given by ticket, and we were able again this year to give a quarter of a lb of tea to each person who received a ticket for bread. We wish it to be clearly understood that people who are unable to attend the service must send a reasonable excuse for their absence, if they wish to receive a ticket." (Warlingham and Chelsham Parish Magazine)

1940   The 1st Canadian Divisional Signals put on two Christmas parties for the children of Bletchingley, partly funded by the men and partly by the officers. 165 under-tens were entertained in the morning and 200 over ten in the afternoon. The entertainments included gifts from Santa Claus and 'Mickey Mouse' films.

22nd 1613   William Woode of Chelsham accused William Haywarde and eight others of, on this night, "entering into his grounde.. ..killing and taking away his conyes and assaulting beating and wounding his servants." (Bostock Fuller J.P.)

1870   "No little excitement was caused when the poll took place in Upper Caterham School, respecting the proposal of the Metropolitan Asylum Board to divert the path from the Asylum to Chaldon. The poll commenced at one o'clock and closed at eight, the result being:- for the Asylum Committee's proposal 81; against 41; majority for the proposal 40." *(Croydon Advertiser)*

1946   The third day of five days of "Carol singing. Whites provided the transport - waggon and two horses, poor things!, £31-s-d was collected for the General Fund. Everyone enjoyed themselves." (Minute Book of St Nicholas Youth Fellowship, Godstone)

23rd 1608   Wylliam Bowyer was bound over to be of good behaviour until he appeared at the next Quarter Sessions where he was "to answere to the hunting chasing and kylling of Conyes in the grounds of John Haywarde of Warlingham." (Bostock Fuller J.P.)

1903   Letter of thanks sent to Mrs Church of Warlingham by the Lady Superintendent of the East End Parish of Plaistow—"Dear Madam, The

Vicar thanks you very much for the beautiful clothes made by the little girls of the Warlingham Sewing Class, and sent by you. Kindly convey a message to the children how thankful the Vicar is and how much the poor people here value the well-made garments. The parcel safely arrived today and gave great satisfaction. - Believe me, dear madam, very truly yours, LADY SUPERINTENDENT." (Warlingham and Chelsham Parish Magazine)

1940   The ladies of Bletchingley responded to the Canadians' generosity (see 21st December 1940) by throwing a party for the troops in the village hall.

24th   1829   The Bletchingley churchwardens paid £2.10s towards the costs of the distribution of two fat oxen, which were the gift of John Perkins Esq. (and helpers), to the poor.

1920   *The Croydon Advertiser* reported on an item of "Feminine Foolishness: For being incapably drunk in Brighton Road, Purley, on Christmas Eve, Alice Goring (54) of Lansdowne Road, Purley, was fined 5s and 7s 6d medical fee. In falling to the ground she badly cut her head for which reason she was unable to appear at the court on Boxing Day."

1940   Caterham and Warlingham's Red to White A.R.P. Log Book records that when the All Clear Air Raid Message White was received at 01.26 the "Woldingham Siren did not operate - instructed Post F.1. to sound ancillary siren. 01.43: Siren sounded all clear Woldingham. 01.50: Situation report to Surrey Control. 02.05: Post Office informed of breakdown of siren at Woldingham."

25th   1615   "I sent William Potter of Oxsted to the House of Correction....he went on Xmas daye." (Bostock Fuller J.P.)

1739   Bletchingley churchwardens "pd the Ringers on Crismas Day 5s."

1812   In Coulsdon the burials took place of Samuel Sellis, 57, and Thomas Charter, 58, both "from the workhouse."

1919   "On Xmas day we had a ramble in search of flowers, finding over 40 species in flower altogether. The freshest specimens of all were those of the Yarrow primrose, wild chervil and violet. The speedwells were in great quantity as were also the mayweeds and winter cress. What a fine show the catkins of hazel now make! And the hips now show out in glorious array." (Arthur Beadell's Nature Notes)

26th   1724   The parish register records that "Sweet William & Black-ey'd Susan: alias William Blackman and Susan Humfrey, both of this Parish of Warlingham, were married by Banns."

1892   "Lovely day. Not many people about here - so very cold. Men at dung cart all day." (Beech Farm Diaries)

27th 1892 "Beautiful Day. Men at dung cart all day. Mr Spenser from the County Council called here to make enquiries about the labourers' wages etc." (Beech Farm Diaries)

1983 A Scouts' boomerang-flying contest was held in Whyteleafe Recreation Ground.

28th 1843 At a meeting of the parishoners of Chipstead "It was resolved that the meeting have great satisfaction in reporting to the Board of Guardians that not one able-bodied man dependent on them for support is at present out of employment and they beg further to express their determination to find employment for their labourers throughout the winter at fair wages, namely from 10 to 13 shillings per week."

29th 1409 John Aynescombe was fined 2d at the manor court in Farleigh for cutting down an oak tree without permission and taking it to Warlingham.

1811 In Sanderstead John Holloway, son of Joseph and Sophia, was baptised. The entry in the parish register is annotated: "N.B.- These people being travellers, their Marriage is doubtful."

30th 1922 At St Nicholas' Church in Godstone a Peal of Superlative Surprise Major was rung, the 5,376 changes taking 3 hours and 12 minutes.

1940 In Caterham there was held an "Identification parade re brawl in Valley Hotel in which some members of 'B' Coy were involved." (War Diary B Coy No.5 Field Ambulance R.C.A.M.C.)

1955 Mr Baedeker U.E. Ramage (see 21st November 1955) wrote again to Coulsdon and Purley's Chief Librarian enclosing a photograph of the inside of the barn at the farm at Purley Oaks, taken in about 1924, and a sketch of the carving on the possible old gibbet post. He says that if it came "from a house, it is curious that the post should be in such a rough state, not even adzed, apart from a well finished carving." *(Plate XXIVb)*

31st 1553 Anne of Cleves signed a receipt to Sir Thomas Cawarden "for one quarter of a year's rent due unto us", this being eight pounds thirteen shillings and ninepence paid "in full contentation, satisfaction, and payment of our rents at Bletchingly, and our lands there."

1924 Purley and District War Memorial Hospital's accounts for the year ended today show a total income of £3,718 13s 2d, of which £1,564 came as payments from patients. Expenditure totalled £2,408 2s 5d and included £841 7s 5d spent on food, £457 10s 4d on Surgery and Dispensary costs and £84 2s 8d spent on the hospital's garden.

1927 According to the *Daily Express* the main road from Croydon to Warlingham was like a glacier, with "8 ft Waves of Ice".

MAIN SOURCES

General: Church Histories.

Local History collections in Purley and Caterham Libraries.

Manorial records (with thanks to Mary Saaler for her translations of the mediaeval Latin originals.)

Parish Magazines.

Parish records.

Probate Inventories and numerous publications, booklets, programmes and general paper ephemera in the East Surrey Museum.

State papers in the Public Record Office.

War Diaries and Intelligence Summaries of Canadian units stationed in the area in World War II, used by kind permission of the Historical Resources Branch of the National Archives of Canada.

Bourne Society publications:

Una Broadbent & R. Latham (Editors)—*Coulsdon Downland Village.*
John Greenwood—*History of Woldingham and Marden Park.*

Mary Saaler—*East Surrey Manors: a Guide to Their Documentation.*
Peter R. Skuse—*A History of Whyteleafe.* (The extracts of the Log Books of the Maple Road Schools are taken from this book.)

Bourne Society Bulletins.

Local History Records.

Souvenir Programme of the Commemoration of the First Centenary of the Opening of the Caterham Railway.

Other publications:

Aviation News.

D.A. Bayliss—*Retracing the First Public Railway.*

Arthur Beadell—*Nature Notes of Warlingham and Chelsham.*

Richard Bell—*The White House Club 50 years on - an historical record.*

David Burns—*The Sheriffs of Surrey.*

J.S. Cooper—*The Old Coulsdon Cricket Club.*

Bostock Fuller J.P.—*Notebook of a Surrey Justice.* (The extracts used appeared in an article by Granville Leveson-Gower in the 1888 *Surrey Archaeological Collections.*)

The Croydon Advertiser and other local and national newspapers.

Croydon Natural History and Scientific Society—*Proceedings and Transactions.*

M. Davison and I. Currie—*Surrey in the Hurricane.*

M. Davison and I. Currie—*The Surrey Weather Book.*

A. Eyles and K. Skone—*The Cinemas of Croydon.*

T. Harding—*Twelve Hours Perambulations or the Rural Beauties of Sanderstead exemplified in a cursory description of that village.*

M. Huitson—*The Story of Caterham and District Gas Company.*

Ald. H. Keatley-Moore—*Croydon and the Great War.*

The Log Books of Kenley National School and Kenley Primary School, used by kind permission of Mrs P. Griffiths, Head Teacher, Kenley Primary School.

S.J. Madge—*Coulsdon Records: The Principal Lands of Coulsdon and Purley and their Holders.*

C.A.F. Meekings and D. Crook (Editors)—*The 1235 Surrey Eyre.*

H.M. Morris—*History of Merstham.* (The excerpts from the Diary of Mrs William Jolliffe are taken from those used in this book. The original Diary is in Taunton Record Office.)

The Travels Through England of Dr Richard Pococke.

Hubert E. Pounds—*Notes on the Birds of Farleigh and District and the North Downs, Surrey.*

C.E. Pringle—*A History of Chipstead.*

Revd Robert Resker—*The History and Development of Purley.*

Capt. F.J. Roberts—*The Wipers Times.*

William B. Robison—*The National and Local Significance of Wyatt's Rebellion in Surrey* (article in *The Historical Journal.*)

William B. Robison—*Murder at Crowhurst: a Study in Early Tudor Law Enforcement* (article in *Criminal Justice History.*)

St Nicholas Church, Godstone—Peal Book.

St Nicholas Youth Fellowship, Godstone—Minute Book.

C.P. Stacey and Barbara M. Wilson—*The Half-Million: The Canadians in Britain 1939-1946.*

Surrey Archaeological Collections.

W.J. Tharby—*The History of Coulsdon West.*

Victoria County History.

Warlingham and District Horticultural Society First Hundred Years.

Alfred L. Whealler—*The Cradle of a Great Corporation.*

Solomon Windross of Beech Farm in Chelsham—his Diaries.